# AMPLIFY

## RAISE YOUR VOICE, BOOST YOUR BRAND AND GROW YOUR BUSINESS

## RONSLEY SERIOJO VAZ

*'Ronsley Seriojo Vaz is a unique human being. Whatever he does, he does really well. He thinks differently, he acts different, he is different. And now he is sharing his knowledge on harnessing the power of conversation to grow a business. Ronsley is leading the global content charge in so many ways. Challenging the status quo, asking the hard questions and always looking for ways to do what we do better, smarter and with more impact. My advice is simple: when Ronsley talks, listen.'*

**— ANDREW GRIFFITHS, AUSTRALIA'S #1
SMALL BUSINESS AND ENTREPRENEURIAL AUTHOR**

*'We've generated a clear, $60,000, $70,000 as a result of working with Amplify for just over three months. If I was to walk down the street and try and talk to someone about buying a $16,000, 40-week program that's going to help position them as a Key Person of Influence, I'm going to have to really, really sell that person. And I'm going to have to talk to them about all those basic ideas. The beauty of what Amplify does for us is that they create a whole content marketing echo chamber of assets. I couldn't recommend Amplify more.'*

**— GLEN CARLSON, CO-FOUNDER OF DENT.GLOBAL**

*'I can tell you directly my podcast and Ronsley have brought me over $80,000 worth of business. Clearly commercially it's been worth it, but for me the worth in question extends beyond the commercial return.'*

**— DR JESSE GREEN, THE SAAVY DENTIST PODCAST**

'

*'For a long time I felt like my business was a million piece puzzle without the picture on the box. But today Ronsley drew me a picture. A clear, beautiful picture that brought all of those floating pieces together into one product eco system. I'm still scrambling under the couch looking for a few missing pieces, wondering if the dog ate some, but tonight, for the first time, I know what the overall puzzle of my business looks like. So thank you Ronsley!'*

**— DR LEANDRA BRADY-WALKER,**
**AUTHOR OF THE COSMOPOLITAN HIPPY**

*'Finally, a book on business expansion that won't ever go out date. I had the pleasure of reading the first few copies and I received more actionable creativity, branding and content marketing tools in this book in the first three chapters than the last five books I read on marketing combined. The strategies are powerful and innovative and most importantly, the delivery of the advice is delicious and makes the entire process of content marketing, business growth and brand equity achievable rather than overwhelming.'*

**— AMBER HAWKEN, AUTHOR OF THE UNFU\*KWITHABLE LIFE**

*'I thought I knew what content creation was, then I read Amplify. Finding your point of intersection and then having a systemic approach to how you can build a business (and brand) on the back of great content is hugely useful. I did have to be in the right headspace to read it, but once I was there I spent two days working through, making copious notes and starting to create a new vision. It's a hugely useful read for anyone in business looking to truly take the next step up.'*

**— MICHAEL BROMLEY, MANAGING DIRECTOR, EA INTERNATIONAL**

First published in 2016 by Grammar Factory
© Ronsley Seriojo Vaz 2016

National Library of Australia Cataloguing-in-Publication entry:
    Creator: Ronsley Vaz, author
    Title: Amplify: Raise your voice, boost your brand and grow your business / Ronsley Vaz
    ISBNs: 9780992317621 (Paperback); 9780992317638 (eBook)

Subjects:
    Marketing.
    Branding (Marketing)
    Business enterprises--Growth.
    Success in business.
Dewey Number: 658.872

Printed in Australia by Excite Print
Book production by Grammar Factory
Editorial services by Grammar Factory
Cover design by Designerbility

**Disclaimer**

# CONTENTS

# SUPPORTING GIRLS' EDUCATION

*Free to Shine believe children should be in schools, not brothels. Through Amplify's partnership with Free to Shine, buying this book will educate a girl in Cambodia for a week.*

*Share the cause, and your contribution, at:*
*theamplifybook.com/share*

# ACKNOWLEDGEMENTS

For Ricardo and Lafira, who did the best they could to deal with a rebel like me.

Thank you dad for setting the example of what it is like to be an entrepreneur; for your constant push to do the right thing and to be resilient in the face of obstacles. Mum, I thank you for the self-confidence you've taught me and for the sense of responsibility that you knocked into me. Because of you, I know that everything that happens in my world is a result of me. Because of you, I will not be a victim to my circumstances.

A special thanks to Andrew Griffiths, Leandra Brady-Walker and Clarissa Rayward for your deep friendship and support. You help me see the world in a new light every time we have a conversation. To the Key Person of Influence community who keep raising the bar for what is possible. To my team at Amplify, and especially to Katherine Cooper for helping get stuff out of my head and onto paper.

I would like to thank Sara, Julia and Jacqui for making this book possible. Sara, you have helped me sound smarter than I actually am.

To Ryder, Roanna, Matt, Allison, Mike, Glen, Dan, Katherine, Jason, Amber, Kristie and the members of the Batman Group; your support through the tough times is what helped define what I could achieve.

To my first clients who gave me their money and believed that I could deliver on my promise. And, to all the potential clients who said 'no', you've helped me improve, get better and try again.

And finally, to my beautiful wife, Rochelle. My greatest victory has been getting you to sign on our marriage certificate. You are my compass. The apple of my eye and the pain in my backside (just kidding). Thank you for believing in me, especially when I didn't believe in myself.

# FOREWORD

Had Alicia Keys been around 100 years ago, she would have been a piano bar singer at best. Back then the radio was the only means of mass communication and it wasn't being used for soul music. Her awesome voice would have filled the cavern of a small room, entertaining a few dozen people each night before she headed home to the modest little flat her tips could afford. No matter how good her voice was, she had no ability to reach a wider audience.

Even fifty years ago, her chances of success in the music industry wouldn't have been good. A few music industry bosses controlled who went into the studio, who could record an album and who got featured on radio. Her chances of getting the green light to perform and record her music would be one in a million.

Fortunately for Alicia Keys, she was born at a time where her talent could be discovered, recorded and distributed to millions of people. As a result, she's built a global brand and made millions of dollars doing what she loves.

Today the cost of recording and distributing anything has dropped to almost zero and no one is standing in the way of a global audience. If you have a message, you've been born at the exact right time in history for that message to spread. You don't need to be talking to people one at a time or waiting for your fifteen minutes of fame on

TV, you can be pumping out content weekly to people all over the world and building an audience or even a movement.

Podcasting is at the heart of this technology revelation. It offers the ability to reach people directly for an extended length of time, and to share big ideas that take more than a few seconds to explain. In a world full of tweets and whirling status updates, podcasts are one of the few mediums that people tune in to for hours at a time.

This offers a remarkable opportunity for you as an entrepreneur. For very little cost you can reach thousands of people with a powerful message, and you don't need to make it fit into 140 characters.

This is important because trust takes time to build. The human brain likes to experience hours of contact with a person before it relaxes into a more trusting relationship. Up until recently, building trust with people meant meeting face to face for long chats. Now the same outcome can be achieved through digital media.

Human brains don't care that it's media either. In 2016, the world mourned the loss of many celebrities who passed away in rapid succession. Despite never actually meeting David Bowie, Prince or Muhammad Ali, people felt they had lost someone close to them because they had consumed hours of media from that person.

As we catapult into the digital age, every entrepreneur, leader and business needs to harness the power of media or get left behind. The customer who loves you today can easily fall in love with a new provider if they discover the right video, book or audio conversation. Don't do it out of obligation though, be sure that you harness the power of media for the right reasons – you see the opportunity in it.

The book you have in your hands is designed for you to see the opportunity in being more media savvy. It gives you a place to start that is low cost, high impact and then it shows you ways to scale your influence.

Like me, you've probably been overwhelmed with the negative news that seems to spew endlessly into our awareness. The business of news networks is to deliver eyeballs to advertisers and they know that negative rapid-fire news gets more response than positive conversations that take time.

You're not running that sort of business and therefore you have the luxury of being free to create positive media that tells a more empowering narrative. You don't need to rush it; you can make your points clearly and powerfully and take all the time you need. Never forget how fortunate you are to be living in a time where all this is possible, in many ways it's your obligation to create content that improves the world and enhances people's lives.

This is a book that will lead to you living a new kind of life. No longer will you perform to a few people and hope to survive; instead you will have a pathway to your global audience and the fortunes that can be unlocked in these magical times we live in. You'll have more value, more influence and more opportunities as a result of what you are about to read.

– Daniel Priestley, co-founder of Dent Global and bestselling author of *Key Person of Influence, Entrepreneur Revolution* and *Oversubscribed*

# INTRODUCTION

*'The first rule of any technology used in a business is that automation applied to an efficient operation will magnify the efficiency. The second is that automation applied to an inefficient operation will magnify the inefficiency.'*

— BILL GATES

**HOW CAN YOU** create a marketing system that enables you to grow as a business with the least amount of effort?

Having been bitten by the entrepreneurial bug, this was the question that annoyed me the most. Over the years, I collected a variety of designations, which include software engineer, software quality manager, tutor, financial advisor, restaurateur, chef, business owner, restaurant manager, bartender, podcaster, speaker and, now, author. I took part in different industries, negotiation standpoints, marketing struggles, c-suite egos and a variety of business challenges. But the biggest challenge remained the one above.

One of the most interesting things I've ever done is interview my dad on my podcast. In that interview, when I asked him if he wished I did something different, he reluctantly said that he wished I did something in 'my field'. He said that with two

Masters' degrees from two different Australian universities, I should have been well-placed to build a computer business. Which is true. However, I've refused to play in one field. I don't really associate myself with any one type of industry. I believe that I am a learner. A generalist. I am a person with shiny-ball syndrome, sure. But, most importantly, I am an entrepreneur.

I am one of those people who loves to put themselves in uncomfortable situations to challenge the status quo and bring a bunch of people together over that situation. Whether it was opening a restaurant that merged Portuguese flavours with Indian spices, or creating the first podcasting conference in the Southern Hemisphere, I loved bringing people together over a new theme and talking about it. And therein lay the answer to the question.

Speech is powerful. Think about every single change in human history. Whether it is race equality or having a phone with one button, we can all trace the big shift to a speech that moved a mass of people to make change possible. As a business owner, how many great conversations have you had in the last month that you just wish you recorded?

When I first got to Australia, if you told me that, as a person of Indian origin, my biggest asset would be my voice, I would have politely asked you to stop making fun of the way I speak. I would have tried extremely hard to sound more Australian and not be seen as a stereotypical Indian with an IT background who drove a cab while I went through university.

As it stands today, because of my podcast, I have a global audience in 133 countries and have developed relationships with over 200 brilliant people who have been guests on my show. That is 200 different perspectives on business and entrepreneurship, and works out to about four one-hour conversations a week for the last two years.

A lot of these people are hard to reach, busy business owners who would not have given me any of their time in another situation. While I was building these relationships with potential partners, I established a team and took the best bits of those conversations to create a marketing system that would not only get my business the right kind of attention, but also the right kind of engagement. The engagement that takes an innocent bystander from lead to customer.

So, despite having written a thesis on software quality systems, I am less than surprised that my book is on marketing and business growth.

# THE PROBLEMS WITH GROWING A BUSINESS

There are six key problems that businesses face. Chances are, you do not face all six of them. You could be going through only one or two. Or you could be going through five. Regardless, these are the issues that stunt growth. As a result of having these problems, we make a bunch of mistakes. And this book is here to correct them.

Businesses are struggling because they are:

1. Vague

2. Nameless

3. Constrained

4. Invisible

5. Stereotypical

6. Naive

I'm not saying this is who you are. And I'm not saying this is who your business is either. I'm saying these are the problems that businesses face today, and, for whatever reason, we don't really pay attention to them. Let's go through them in more detail so you can see what I'm talking about.

# #1. VAGUE

This is probably one of the biggest issues. When a business owner suffers from this problem, there are three things that they won't be able to answer properly:

1. Who they are and what makes them different.

2. Who their audience is.

3. Who their peers are.

So why, exactly, should you figure out these things? Because if you don't know who you are, and what makes you different, there's no reason for people to choose you over your competition. If you don't know who your audience is, you won't be able to find them or help them. And if you don't know who your peers are, you'll never find anyone to partner with.

# #2. NAMELESS

If you have the first issue, then you definitely have the second, which is being nameless. Basically, this means your messaging cannot be recognised without a logo being attached to it. You see this a lot these days. How many times have you noticed photographers put their branding at the bottom of images? They do that because, otherwise, you wouldn't be able to tell them apart from each other.

There are, however, exceptions. I know one photographer – his name is Jason Malouin – who never puts his logos on his images. Why? Because you can recognise a Jason Malouin shot from a mile away.

If you think that the only way someone will recognise your messaging is from a label saying it is by you, then you're nameless. So we've got to find a way to make you 'known'.

# #3. CONSTRAINED

This is a common issue, especially for businesses that have established and developed a product market fit. You're doing something right in that you have customers, you have money coming in the door and you have transactions happening, but you have no room to grow.

This is what I mean by constrained. When the business first started, you didn't think about growth – you didn't think about scaling. This means there are no systems in place that allow the business to grow without adding new staff. So you hire new staff.

Why is that a mistake? You might think that the only way to grow a business is to add new staff. But that's an ego thing. The number of staff really makes no difference to how good you are as a business. At the end of the day, new staff might mean more customers, but if they still give you the same bottom line in terms of profit, then you have an issue. You're constrained. You have an issue with scaling. You have an issue with growth.

# #4. INVISIBLE

Getting overlooked happens a lot. Why? There's so much advertising out there. There's so much marketing out there. You might as well be invisible.

Now, when you think about how people buy today, when they have an issue, they search for it. If they can't find you when they're searching for it, you'll be overlooked. If you're spending money to be heard, to be seen, and you're still being overlooked, you're making a mistake somewhere. Businesses are overlooked because they don't have authentic and consistent content to attract the right people to them.

# #5. STEREOTYPICAL

This is the other end of the problem – if people are finding you when they search their issue, but still not engaging with you, you're being dismissed. Why? Because you're stereotypical. They don't trust you.

When I say stereotypical, I think you're trying, too often, to do what everyone else is doing. What that really means is that you have no platform where your clients can spend time with you. So when someone comes across you as a business, they're just not going to buy from you. You've got to spend time with them for them to trust you, for them to know you, for them to like you. If they don't like you, know you, trust you – if you're just a stereotype, like everyone else, doing what everyone else is doing – they're not going to buy from you.

You might even be trying to copy other businesses, looking at what other people are doing, saying, 'Oh that guy has just got an amazing podcast, let me start a podcast,' or, 'That person has had really good success with television advertising, so let me spend $100,000 on a new television ad.' That kind of stuff doesn't work, because trying to copy another business that isn't you, that doesn't have the same audience as you, and that doesn't have the same peers or partners as you, is just a big, big mistake. It's not going to solve your problem.

# #6. NAIVE

Businesses tend to be naive when it comes to measurement. Usually, they have no real way to measure if they're getting a return on investment when it comes to their marketing money.

Think about radio as an example. Normal FM radio will tell you that they have a broadcast reach of X amount of people. But do you really think that X amount of people are tuning in at the same time to listen to your ad? Even if they are listening to your ad, do you have a way to measure how many of those people it will attract to your business? We don't actually have a way to measure the return on investment.

If your business is naive, you may find yourself paying lots of money for immeasurable marketing, with no idea whether you're seeing a return. Consider billboards, for example, where someone tells you your reach in terms of people driving past. What they don't tell you is that most of those people are on their phones, and not seeing your advertising at all.

Another naïve move is being overprotective of your ideas. This is probably the worst approach in today's world, because every bit of information is freely available. And the businesses that are open to sharing are the ones that develop trust quicker. Think about how quickly Wikipedia overthrew Microsoft Encarta in the encyclopaedia arena. Think about all the open source software that you use, like Gmail. It works. The advantages of collaboration are lost if we don't share because we are thinking that some other person is going to take our idea and make millions of dollars with it.

If business growth is an issue, chances are, you're facing one of these six problems, and making the bunch of mistakes that go along with them. All the while, you know something isn't working, but you don't know what or why, so you throw money at the business, in all the wrong spots. You let ego seep into your marketing, for example, putting an ad in an in-flight magazine just so you can say your business is in there. You work longer hours trying to improve things, and burn out.

This book is for the business owner who realises that there must be a better way to grow their business. For the lover of business who understands that there are areas where the least amount of effort will yield the most results. The entrepreneur who believes in Pareto's principle and knows that the 80-20 rule is not a myth but a truth. This book is for the business owner who wants each of their people, from potential customers to preferred partners, from loyal fans to team members, to see why they love what they do.

# AMPLIFY YOUR BUSINESS

After working with a variety of different organisations, from small businesses with a few team members to large ones that are listed on stock exchanges, I've established that there are three main aspects to marketing any business. You need to get attention. Turn that attention into engagement. Then take that engagement and nurture it into sales.

In the coming chapters, I will challenge you to tell me who your business is. And I will take you through the seven-step AMPLIFY framework that overcomes these problems and enables a business to get attention, engagement and sales.

| | |
|---|---|
| **A** | Analyse your audience |
| **M** | Mould your brand |
| **P** | Productise your ecosystem |
| **L** | Launch audio |
| **I** | Intensify your message |
| **F** | Foster engagement |
| **Y** | Yield on investment |

This framework enables you to remove the difficult sales conversations from your business. The ones that arise when you meet someone for the first or second time and expect them to buy from you. Whether you are looking to break through a crowded market or lead a new one, and whether you offer a product or provide a service, this system works.

# A — ANALYSE YOUR AUDIENCE

Once you know who your audience is, you will be able to express yourself. You won't be vague with your messaging any more. You'll know exactly who you are, exactly who you're after and exactly who you can partner with.

# M — MOULD YOUR BRAND

Your brand is not just a logo strapped across your website. It is about being recognisable for things that you do, things that you say. You are not nameless any more; you are recognised because of how you interact. Consistent branding is so important. It includes how you treat your people, how you treat your customers. It includes how you treat your peers. And it includes how you market your business.

# P — PRODUCTISE YOUR ECOSYSTEM

I'm going to talk about your product ecosystem because it's probably one of the most important things involved in scaling a business. If you don't have a product ecosystem, you're not going to be able to grow your business without adding more staff and throwing more resources at the problem.

# L – LAUNCH AUDIO

I'm a huge believer in audio. When someone sees you on television, before you even open your mouth, before you even have anything to say, people will look at you and judge you based on how you're dressed, on how you look, on what your hairstyle is, before they even judge the words coming out of your mouth. That does not happen in audio. And if you don't have an audio platform today, I promise you that's going to be a problem five years from now. An audio platform is the only form of content where someone can consume you while they're doing something else. They don't have to stop what they're doing, so you won't have the issue of being overlooked any more. You won't be stereotypical – it's a platform where you can be different.

# I – INTENSIFY YOUR MESSAGE

This part is the meat and potatoes. This is the part where everything comes together and makes a massive splash. I will show you how to take this authentic content that you've created through your audio platform and put it across every other platform. Every single aspect will be consistent in your messaging. You will be marketable, you will be visible, and it will no longer be possible to dismiss you.

# F — FOSTER ENGAGEMENT

Once you get attention, chances are, you can get engagement. So I'm going to show you how intensifying your marketing will get the right attention, and then I'm going to show you how to get the engagement. Because we know that a customer needs to know, like and trust us before they buy from us. I'm going to show you how to foster engagement and turn it into sales, revenue and growth.

# Y — YIELD ON INVESTMENT

All this stuff that you're doing needs to be measured. Yield on investment is about how we can take that measurement, improve on it, and stop being naive about where we're spending our money. We're going to talk about what the right metrics are, why they matter, and how you can regularly improve on your strategy.

The AMPLIFY framework enables you to create a system that gains you fifteen times the impact with a tenth of the hard work. It takes your best stories, thoughts and ideas and magnifies them. So, when you tell your peers that you have found a marketing system that allows you to grow as a business with the least amount of effort, it is a statement that you can take to the bank.

# CHAPTER 1

# ANALYSE YOUR AUDIENCE

*'The first step in exceeding your customer's expectations is to know those expectations.'*

— ROY H. WILLIAMS

I KNOW BUSINESS owners. What they want the most is for potential customers to contact them and ask for help, saying, 'Please help me solve this problem. I know you're the best person to do it.' There's no better feeling than someone doing that. Because the competition becomes irrelevant.

The secret to this is knowing who your potential customers are and expressing yourselves to them. Let me give you an example. Clint Salter (clintsalter.com), a speaker at We Are Podcast 2016, is amazing at what he does. The reason I contacted him and asked him to speak at We Are Podcast conference is because he's so good at knowing his audience. If you go to his website, the first line that you see is: 'Are you a dance studio owner? Learn how to grow, promote and profit from your studio.' In that first line, you know exactly what he does and whom he's trying to help. So if you're a dance studio owner, where do you think you're going to click? If you're a dance studio owner, why wouldn't you learn how to grow, promote and profit from your studio? The reason you want to find out more is because he's so specific. He's done his analysis, he knows what he stands for, he knows what makes him special as a mentor, and he knows whom he's helping. It's brilliant when you get to a point where you know exactly whom it is that will benefit from your services.

So let me ask you this: If he knows that he's helping dance studio owners, don't you think he knows exactly where these people exist? As an example, dance studio owners need a whole bunch of equipment for their dance studio, so he partners with the equipment store, and the people who deal with fit out for new dance studios, and he's got his people straight away.

A lot of you reading this right now might say, 'Well, how many dance studio owners are there on the planet?' And that's the point. Even though there are relatively few, who is the most influential when it comes to mentoring a dance studio owner? It's Clint, who is known as a speaker and author as well as a mentor. When you're reading his website, he tells you: 'My goal is to have your business reach more customers through holistic marketing strategies that boost sales, create lifetime customers and quite simply make a difference to you, your staff and the customers you serve.' Very plain, very simple, very succinct. Clint is the perfect example of how analysing your audience helps you express yourself. He's not vague; there's no chance that, in those sentences, you'll not understand what he means.

So what do you need to do to express yourself? You need to analyse your people. And when I talk about your people, I'm talking about your team, I'm talking about your potential clients, and I'm also talking about your peers. Because, trust me, no business is an island. Somehow, we can forget to incorporate our peers into the analysis, but they're so important. When you think about successful people, and you think about the people they have around them, they always have influential friends. So your peers are as important as your potential clients.

And how do you do it? You have got to find out who you are. You have got to find out who your people are and the best questions to ask them. And you've got to understand what to do with that information.

Step number one is crucial. In fact, it is so crucial that you'll see it come up in every chapter. Every single thing that you do from this point onwards is hinged on you analysing your audience and analysing them properly. It is key.

There's this amazing TED Talk by Matt Chan. If you get a chance, Google it. He's the creator of the American television show Hoarders, and he has this amazing talk on how storytelling is so important, and how you can tell someone a story and capture their imagination, capture their attention – but, however brilliant the story is, and however fantastically it is structured, none of that matters if you don't know who your audience is. None of that matters if you're telling your story to people who don't really care about the subject.

You need to find the right audience for your subject. What's your subject? That's about who you are and what you do.

# START WITH YOU

So let's start with you. Like when you sit in a plane and they tell you to fit your own oxygen mask before you help anyone else, it's really important that you figure out who you are as a business owner, and, as a result, what your business stands for, in order to figure out who your people are. If you don't know who *you* are, figuring out who your people are is an exercise of putting the cart before the horse.

What makes you you? Businesses always tell you what they do, and sometimes how they do it, but they very rarely tell you why they do what they do. If you figure out a way to communicate your message in a way that says why you do what you do, followed by how you do it and what you do, then it has more of an impact, because it talks directly to the way the brain works.

## RECOMMENDED RESOURCE

Simon Sinek wrote a brilliant book called *Start With Why* where he shares how a strong why can transform your business. As he argues, people don't buy *what* you do; they buy *why* you do it.

As an example, think about someone who has a health food store. If they're asked what it is that they do, chances are, they're going to say that they're a health food store. They might go to the extent of telling people that they're a health food store that specialises in weight loss products.

However, what if they actually said, 'We believe that people should not have to struggle with weight loss. There is an option, right now, for them to get their weight under control, and they can do that with the brilliant products we stock. By the way, we are a health food store.'? That has a different impact to saying, 'We're a health food store that stocks weight loss products.'

All this thought around 'Why?' starts with you, with what you believe in. Everything that the business does going forward, everything that your team does going forward, stems from you. You need to figure out what it is that makes you unique, what makes you so different to everyone else.

Chances are, there are competitors in your field providing the same service. But they're not you. They don't have the same experiences, the same insight, the same perspective, which have brought you to the point where you created your own business.

There is no better way to figure out what makes you happy and what makes you tick than starting with your values. This isn't necessarily easy, because we take our highest values – the things that we're great at – for granted. We take all that comes naturally to us for granted, because it comes so easily. To figure out our values, it helps to have some intimate conversations with people who are close to us. I'll give you an example from when I went through the exercise of trying to figure out who I am.

The Demartini workbook took me 3.5 hours to complete, after which I asked my wife Rochelle 'do you know what my highest value is?' She didn't even look up. She just said, 'Freedom.' It took me 3.5 hours on my own to figure out that my highest value was freedom, when the people around me – the people closest to me – already knew what made me tick.

## RECOMMENDED RESOURCE

Dr John Demartini, the author of *The Gratitude Effect* and over forty other books, created a really cool workbook about determining your highest values. The workbook, called *Determining Values*, asks you a bunch of different questions to help you figure out what your highest values are.

I strongly suggest to you that you have these conversations with people, and find out what it is that you pay most attention to. What is it that you do that only you do? What are those traits that make you so unique that other people around you love – or even hate – you for them? Gun to your head, what is most important to you? What gives you most energy? When you look back on your life, and you reminisce about the things that you've done, what makes you most happy?

Look at how you spend your time. Look at things that have made you happy in the past. Look at what circumstances have brought you most joy, even going back to when you were a kid. Think about what activity you could spend hours and hours doing and not really care about whether you get paid or not. Not really care whether it's being productive or not. Not really care about whether it's the best use of your time. Just be really happy doing it. What is it?

Once you've identified your values, figure out your intersection – where two of your highest values meet. Let me give you some examples. If you think about Steve Jobs, his intersection is liberal arts and technology. Everything that he did in business, in life, centred around liberal arts and technology, whether it was Pixar, the Apple Mac, the iPad or the iPhone. When you look at Richard Branson's intersection, it is business and fun. It doesn't matter what business he gets into; as long as he injects fun into it, it becomes the Virgin brand.

For myself, I had a conversation with Glen Carlson. You can find it online on SoundCloud, an audio capture of about thirty minutes of me talking with Glen called 'figuring out my intersection'. I already knew that I loved challenging the status quo and bringing people together over a new concept. The point at which those two things come together is my sweet spot.

Your intersection makes you different. When you figure out what makes you different, it's very easy to figure out what makes your business different, because you bring your traits to your business.

The next stage is to know what your goals are. When you think of yourself as a business owner, what is it that you actually want to be known for? A lot of us have a very fuzzy version of what this actually is. I want to ask you why do you, as a business owner, exist? What do you want your business to achieve? I believe that goals and where you're headed is pivotal. Otherwise, it's like sitting in a car and not knowing where you're going. How exactly are you going to get there?

So where do you see your business in the next year, the next three years, the next five years? What do you want to achieve? What is your vision? What does success look like to you?

Once you know where you want to be – where you're headed – you can break it down into smaller goals that will get you there.

There's no better way to create these goals than using the S.M.A.R.T. framework. I'm not going to reinvent the wheel here – S.M.A.R.T. goals have been around for ages, and are not something I've developed. Using this framework to define your goals is the best way to get clarity around where you're going.

## SMART FRAMEWORK

**S**: It needs to be specific. It needs to be significant. It needs to be stretching. You can take any one of these, but I think specific is the most important one.

**M**: It needs to be measurable. It can be meaningful and motivational as well, but, above all, it needs to be measurable.

**A**: It needs to be attainable. It can also be agreed upon, it can be acceptable, it can be action-oriented, but for me, it needs to be achievable – attainable.

**R**: It needs to be realistic. You can also think about whether it is relevant, reasonable, rewarding and results-oriented. But how realistic is this goal that you've set for yourself?

**T**: It needs to be time-bound. Your goal should be trackable, tangible and timely, but, above all, time-bound. So put a deadline on your goal.

So make a list of goals, and make sure they're S.M.A.R.T.

# YOUR IDEAL CLIENT

Once you figure out who you are and what you want, you need to start looking at who your people are. Very simply, figuring out who your people are means thinking about the client who you could go and have dinner with and spend time with, and you'd enjoy each other's company. Who is this person? What do they do? Why is it so easy for you to get along with them? Why is it so easy for them to get along with you? This, in my opinion, is your ideal client.

Now, there are variations of that ideal client. If you think of a dartboard, the bullseye is your dream client, the person that you love hanging out with, and then you have all the areas around that bullseye that you service as well.

There are a few things that you should look at when you think about your ideal client. First, identify who they are and what their background is. Do an exercise on them similar to the one you just did on yourself.

- Where do they hang out the most?
- What is it that makes them tick?
- Where do they spend their time?
- Where do they spend their energy?
- What do they care about the most?
- What are the things that are bothering them the most?
- What are their biggest problems?

Think about the things that really annoy your ideal client.

- What frustrates them?

- What does your ideal client wish they had more or less of?

When you figure out what they wish they had more of, and what they wish they had less of, you automatically start to think about how you can solve their problems. When you think about the things that frustrate them the most, you automatically start thinking from their point of view, rather than pushing your product onto someone who doesn't even know that your product can help them.

One of the most brilliant questions to have in your back pocket is: 'What does your ideal client secretly fear?' These are the fears that they don't even voice to other people. These are the fears that they think about late at night, when they're alone. If you figure out what they secretly fear, and if you talk to those secret fears, you've suddenly found a common ground on which they can connect with you.

Let's think about someone who's a high-performing individual but doesn't eat right. I'll keep coming back to these kinds of examples because this was something I actually had to think about for a business of my own. So when you think about someone in that position, they secretly fear that their bad eating habits will snowball into a lifestyle change for good, and they will just be known as a person who is unhealthy. They might no longer be seen first and foremost as someone who works a lot and is a great entrepreneur, but as someone who is unhealthy. One of their secret fears is that their bad habits will snowball into heart disease in the future. And one of their secret fears is that they will have to invest in the next size up in clothes, and it really annoys them that they might get to that point because they haven't sorted out their diet.

These high-performing individuals wish that they could complete a marathon, or do something that would really give them this jolt of energy. But they can't, because they're eating badly and they're not in the right shape to even attempt to start training. They wish that they had more energy throughout the day, and didn't necessarily need a coffee and a Red Bull to keep them going. They wish that they really enjoyed their workouts and didn't feel like a workout is a chore.

When you figure this out, then you can work out what their problems are. Their problems are that they don't have time to cook; they don't want to eat food that they don't like, but they don't have time to go to the butcher and buy fresh meat, go to the fruit and vegetable store and buy fruit and vegetables, go to the fishmonger for fresh fish, and then go to the supermarket to do the rest. They don't have the time to do all that shopping and then come home and take the food, put it together and come up with something that they like. Once you understand these problems, you can start to work on solving them.

The more you know your people, the easier it is to go and find them. The easier it is to recognise them when you see them in front of you.

The easier it is for you to speak their language, to relate to them and to help them.

# YOUR PEERS

Once you've analysed your clients, you need to think about your peers. Your peers are important. While they may be your competition, the last way that you should think of them is as people out to get you. I believe in the claim that you're the average of the five people you hang around with the most. So why not hang around with a bunch of people who will raise your game?

Think about very simple traits. If your highest value, for example, is success, and your definition of success is to have a lot of money, the quickest and easiest way to achieve it is for your friends and your peers to be really wealthy people. Whether you like it or not, you will find a way to level up, because otherwise you'll stick out like a sore thumb. Now think about health. If you want to be healthy and you want to feel fit and trim, then you'll best be served by hanging out with people who have a healthy, active lifestyle.

Not only will these people help you level up, but they will also keep you accountable. One of the best things in business is to find a group of people whom you can be accountable to. I believe that my own success over the last few years has come from being accountable to a bunch of people. It doesn't even matter if they're in your industry or not; it just matters that they are business owners and they have a similar path to you. They understand what you're going through.

They understand what your goals are, and they understand what makes a business owner tick. When you have a bunch of people whom you are accountable to, there's no way that you're going to meet them the next time you have an accountability session and say, 'Oh I didn't do what I said I was going to do.' It's like waking up in the morning and looking at the lawn, which hasn't been mown in ages, and saying to yourself, 'I'm going to mow the lawn today.' There's a much higher likelihood of it actually happening if you turn to your partner and say, 'You know what? Today I'm going to mow the lawn.'

When picking peers who will help you level up, ask yourself how they would react in a crisis. Would they give you a space for you to feel sorry for yourself or would they help you look at the positive? My biggest marker for the people that I consider peers is that, when things get tough, they ask me the right questions or say the right things to help me perceive the situation differently. Even if, at the time, the things they say and the questions they ask get me angry. I believe that your peers share similar values to you. In my instance, my peers are so true to their values that they don't mind upsetting others or themselves in the short term, just so that they feel like they have done the right thing. Ask yourself, could you hang out with this person and have a conversation about ideas? Could you disagree on a concept and still have dinner together? Is the trust and respect mutual? These questions are more important than if they share your target market.

Your peers keep you on the straight and narrow. These are the people you might end up partnering with, entering into joint ventures with. The people hanging around in your peer groups might well have access to your ideal clients and your ideal team members as well. So it becomes a very easy way to reach some new clients, and meet some of the people you want on your side. I am not saying that you should make friends with someone only to get to their clients; I'm saying if you spend the time figuring out who your peers are and developing relationships with them, discovering new opportunities is not far off.

So these are the three things that you need to pay attention to when you analyse your audience: who you are, who your clients are and who your peers are. Once you figure out these three things, everything else from this point onwards becomes easier. Everything else is like swimming downstream: your branding, your product ecosystem, your audio, your messaging, your marketing, your engagement and your measurements. They all come back to this first step where you figure out whom it is that you're trying to reach.

Download the worksheets that go with this book at theamplifybook.com.

CHAPTER 2

# MOULD YOUR BRAND

*'Think about what people are doing on Facebook today.
They're keeping up with their friends and family, but they're
also building an image and identity for themselves, which in
a sense is their brand. They're connecting with the audience
that they want to connect to. It's almost a disadvantage if
you're not on it now.'*

**— MARK ZUCKERBERG**

**THE BIGGEST PROBLEM** that we face as business owners is that our
potential customers – and peers who might want to work with us –
haven't heard of us before. This happens so often, because we get lost
within our industry, and we get lost within the services we provide.
Even if they come across you by chance, you still have to convince
them that you're worth your salt.

That makes you nameless. That makes you lost in this sea of other
services, other businesses, other industries. There is this amazing

statistic that we get bombarded by about 5,000 different messages from advertisers and marketers every single day. That's a lot, right? So our brains are now trained to ignore certain things, and it's not necessarily our customers' fault if they easily ignore us; it's our fault for not being easily recognisable. Being recognisable means our potential customers look at our work and think, 'Wait, I know who this person is. I know this business. I know that these guys solve this particular problem, and they do it with these services and products.' We want our customers to recommend us to their friends because our message is so unique and consistent, and they know that we can deliver. We want clients who can't wait to work with us, saying, 'When do you have an availability? You're oversubscribed.'

So, what does all this have to do with branding?

# WHY IS BRANDING SO IMPORTANT?

Branding is how you make a name for yourself. It is how you stand out. It is much more than a logo or a colour scheme or a font. It helps you in a myriad of ways:

## 1. BRANDING PROMOTES RECOGNITION

People tend to do business with people and companies they're familiar with. That's the reason why you see companies spending so much money on advertisements in random places – it's purely because it promotes recognition. When you've become familiar enough with a company over a long period of time, you think, 'I trust that brand.' It's one of those really subconscious things that happen to us as human beings. So if your branding is consistent and easy to recognise, you can help people feel more at ease buying any of your products and services at a later stage.

# 2. YOUR BRAND HELPS SET YOU APART FROM THE COMPETITION

In the current business market, it is critical to stand apart from the crowd. It has never been more important to be different and to challenge the status quo. Just because something's previously been done a certain way, it doesn't mean that that is the way it should be done going forward. You're no longer competing on the local stage; your business is now competing in the global space.

Your brand helps you set yourself apart. Ask yourself on a regular basis, 'How do I stand out from the hundreds and thousands of similar businesses around the world?' and challenge yourself. I think if you can say that you're the first on the planet to do something, that's pretty cool. Then, once you have success in that area, and you set yourself apart, everyone will want to follow. So your branding helps set yourself apart from the competition, because when someone looks at you, your brand, your business and your messaging, they associate you with change, and they associate you with innovation in your industry. So, automatically, you're seen as a leader.

## 3. YOUR BRAND TELLS PEOPLE ABOUT YOUR DNA

This is why it is so important to analyse your audience before you get to the branding exercise. Through your brand, your people get to understand why you do what you do. The full brand experience – from visual elements like the logo and the artwork to the way someone is welcomed into the business – tells your customer a lot about the kind of business and the kind of person you are. So your branding is key.

Ask yourself on a regular basis, 'Are all my points of entry – the points where someone is first exposed to my business – telling the right story?' When someone first sees any messaging that you put up, when someone gets on the phone with you, when someone talks to one of your team members, if you are telling the right story, the one your audience is interested in hearing, then you can invite them to be a part of it.

## 4. YOUR BRAND TELLS YOUR CUSTOMERS WHAT TO EXPECT

A clear brand strategy provides clarity for your potential customers. A brand that is consistent and clear enables them to understand the promises that you're making and puts them at ease. It tells them how to act, it tells them how to win, it tells them how to meet their goals, and it tells them how to tackle their problems and ultimate pain. It tells them how you are going to provide a solution, and how fast. A strong brand tells people what to expect. It represents the promise you make them.

# 5. A STRONG BRAND WINS REFERRALS

Every single business owner would love it if each of their current customers introduced them to one new customer – that would be fantastic, wouldn't it? Well, people love to tell others about brands that they like. They love to tell others about brands that they associate themselves with. So if you find your people and establish a strong brand that they love, you will find this connection.

A strong brand reflects what people believe in. This is why people wear brands, eat brands, listen to brands, get tattooed with brands. There's an emotional attachment – buying is an emotional experience. If they feel good when they consume or buy your brand, then they usually can't wait to tell someone else about it. People are constantly telling others about brands they love, so that they can be a part of it too.

# 6. YOUR BRAND HELPS YOU CREATE CLARITY AND STAY FOCUSED

One of the hardest things in business is not knowing when to say no. You want to say yes to everything. When you have a clear brand, it helps you stay focused. A clear brand strategy helps you stick to your mission and your vision as a business owner. It guides your marketing efforts, your hiring efforts, and it saves you time and money straying from your original goal. Your brand reminds you who you are and where you're going, so you can easily say no to anything that doesn't fit with getting to that destination.

# 7. A STRONG BRAND GENERATES BUSINESS VALUE

A strong brand brings value to your business well beyond your physical assets. When you think about big brands you buy from – Coca Cola, Red Bull, Apple, Ford, Virgin Airlines – all of these companies are worth way more than their equipment, the products in their warehouse and the factories that they own. Their brand is so powerful it has created worth that far exceeds their physical assets.

Think about Beyoncé, as an example, as a brand in herself. If she wears a hat, the company that made it will suddenly become a very profitable hat company, because it's been endorsed by her. It's now worth more than its physical value. A brand that strong even generates business value for the other brands it touches.

I hope I've convinced you that you need to spend time on a branding exercise because too often we, as business owners, get a logo designed and expect to get away with it. Now let's see how you can build your brand.

# HOW TO MOULD YOUR BRAND

In order to brand your business well, you have got to do three things:

1. Establish your brand identity.

2. Identify your brand platforms.

3. Create brand templates.

## 1. ESTABLISH YOUR BRAND IDENTITY

Your brand identity comes from figuring out who you are, what you stand for and who your people are, which we've looked at in the first chapter. To publically establish your identity, you have to think about how you're going to represent it visually. Your logo, your tagline, the colours you use, the images you share – these are all important in terms of recognition, so get a brand strategist on board to figure out exactly how to personify your brand from a visual point of view. Everything should be presented consistently and clearly, in line with the image you want to portray to the world – having a standard way to display yourself is important.

Next, think about the delivery of your copy into the world. From the 'About' page on your website to a letter that you send to a potential client, this is all part of your copy. What tone do you want to use? Think about customer testimonials, case studies, examples – all these things represent your brand and support your identity.

## 2. IDENTIFY YOUR BRAND PLATFORMS

The next thing that you have got to look at is your brand platforms. There are a whole variety of different social media platforms that you can be a part of – any social media strategist will tell you that. But you've got to decide which ones will work best for you based on who your people are. You have got to figure out where they hang out so you can reach them with your message and expose them to your brand.

The idea of this book is to allow you to take a message and amplify it, putting it across all manner of different platforms, but you need to be aware which social media interactions are imperative for your business. What platforms gain you the most traction? Make a list of what they are, and make sure you have a consistent presence across them, coherent with your brand identity.

## 3. CREATE BRAND TEMPLATES

Create templates for everything. Once you have a brand strategist come on board to figure out what your logo is, what your brand colours are and what your fonts are, you can ask them to create a bunch of templates that you can use on different platforms like LinkedIn, Facebook, Twitter … They can format a consistent way to present the titles of your blog posts and quotes across a variety of channels.

Once you have templates, you can just pass them over to your team and they can post relevant content in a consistent manner each time. So create templates for everything.

## RECOMMENDED RESOURCE

If you're creating your own templates, you can use canva.com to create them and then reuse them over and over again.

This whole process makes it easy to represent your brand in a consistent way, but what does this mean in practice? Let's take a closer look at your business and see what improvements you can make to your branding in specific areas.

# FIVE AREAS YOU MIGHT BE MISSING

The reason I put this section together is that we have this idea that branding means colours, it means logos, it means fonts, and it's only the visual aspects that determine your brand. I challenge you to accept that there is much more to it than that. Here are five areas that you may well be missing when it comes to your branding:

# 1. HOW YOU ON-BOARD YOUR CUSTOMERS

Do you have a process when you first get your customers on board? Do you have a way to get them to emotionally attach themselves to the process of change? If you provide a service or a product that takes them from a place of problems to a happier place in which they get those problems solved, then you need to get them invested in a process. Once I started paying attention to the on-boarding of my customers, it made a massive difference to my business.

So how do you on-board your customers? Do you perform the process consistently? Does the process align with what your brand stands for?

# 2. HOW YOU ANSWER THE PHONE AND REPLY TO EMAILS

If you're a brand that's pretty edgy and you answer the phone just like everyone else, then you're missing a trick when it comes to branding your business. If you call yourself the friendliest financial advisor in the country and someone answers the phone and just says, 'Hello,' then that's inconsistent with your branding. Meanwhile, if you consider yourself to be a very professional company, very to-the-book, and your emails come across very blasé, then that's an issue as well. You need to be consistent. What does your email signature say? Is it just a name and number? Does it include colours? Is that signature consistent with what your brand stands for and do you use it consistently? Think about the sheer amount of emails that we send out on a daily basis – you need to make sure there's no mismatch when it comes to branding.

How do you answer the phone? How do you reply to emails? Is it in line with your brand and the promises you're making your people?

# 3. HOW YOU WRITE A BLOG POST

Businesses often outsource their blog, and they give ghostwriters a whole bunch of topics to write for them. Now, if these articles come back and they're not consistent with the brand, people may not know the reason why, but they will realise that something's up. If authenticity is a key value of your brand and you have outsourced your blog, you're in danger of being inauthentic.

Are your blog posts written by yourself or a member of your team, or do you outsource? If the latter, have you provided the writer/s with training around your brand, and do you check that what they write aligns with your brand?

# 4. HOW YOU HOST AN EVENT

When you host an event, you need to pay attention to the idea that your brand stands for something. An event should mark something bigger than just you and your business; otherwise, you've missed a trick.

When you hold an event, does it celebrate your brand and represent who you are? Does it further a cause you believe in? Do the suppliers you work with to throw the event and the people you invite to attend hold the same values and beliefs that are part of your brand? Every aspect of planning and execution involved on the day is a representation of your identity, so make sure that everything and everyone fits.

# 5. HOW YOU HIRE YOUR TEAM

Your team is an extension of you and your business. From the first hire to the most recent hire, their values need to be aligned with your brand. Your team members represent you and are ambassadors of your brand. They are often on the front line, dealing with the people that your business will ultimately serve. So your team can help build or break your brand. Cultural fit is often more important than experience when it comes to staff who will help your business grow. It is much easier to train a willing staff member in relevant skills than alter their beliefs if they run counter to your own.

When you recruit, do you pay attention to the values of your candidates? Do you check that their values are in alignment with yours?

These are just five areas to address which will help you mould a consistent brand. The important thing to remember is that every aspect of your business needs to be aligned with your identity. A strong brand will help you gain recognition, set yourself apart from the competition, communicate your DNA, set expectations, win referrals, stay focused and generate business value, so an exercise in branding is a must.

For a worksheet to help you mould your brand, go to theamplifybook.com

# CHAPTER 3

# PRODUCTISE YOUR ECOSYSTEM

*'Nike doesn't want to make products for everyone – they want to make products for champions.'*

**– SIMON SINEK**

**THIS STEP ALLOWS** you to become scalable. If you feel constrained, if you feel like you're working long hours, if you feel like the only way you can grow is through hiring more people and getting more clients – then this is an important step for you. It's not about increasing your turnover and saying, 'I'm a $1M business,' or 'I'm a $2M business,' not if your profit remains the same, and you're exchanging time for money. At the end of the day, as a business owner, the important thing is that you have **more profit**.

Being scalable means we can create more products and services and still help a bunch of people without necessarily having to add more staff to the equation. I'm not saying that you've got to understaff your business; I'm saying that there is a way to scale your business, because today we have the technology available to us.

Let me tell you about some clients of ours, migration lawyers who are based in Sydney. Their biggest issue was that they were working a ridiculous amount of hours. They had all these clients coming to them, and they didn't know how to deal with the increase, so they hired more people. When they hired more people, they found out that their turnover increased – so the amount of money that the business was making in the year increased – but when it came to their profit, not only did it not stay the same, it actually decreased, because the cost of having new staff members was large, and not matched by the amount of money that they were bringing in.

So they came to us and one of the things that we did for them was develop a product ecosystem. We figured out that their biggest issue as migration lawyers was that every service they offered was a time-for-money exchange. And, unfortunately, most businesses today are structured in the same way. I give you some of my time and you give me some of your money. But with the right technology, the right thought process and the right intent, you don't have to kill yourself trying to make more money. Let me explain.

For these migration agents, we noticed that getting their clients Australian citizenship required the least amount of work. They didn't need to be spending all this time with the clients. It would be possible to tell them exactly where to go, what to download and where to submit it, and they would still get their citizenship, because they were already vetted when they got their permanent residency.

So we developed a citizenship product. It had a five-step method. There was a bunch of explanation videos in there, there were all the forms that they needed, and it cost someone who was looking to get citizenship $379, down from $2,200 – with zero time required of the actual lawyers. So the clients could log in, they could pay the money, and they knew exactly what they needed to download, what forms they needed to attach, how to attach them and where to submit it all – because the videos told them exactly what to do – and they got citizenship.

That has been a massive, massive result for the lawyers, because they've been making in the tens of thousands of dollars every month as a result, and all they do is direct all citizenship enquiries to this course. No need for extra staff or extra time. Meanwhile, the clients love it because it's cheap. No other lawyer was doing it at the time we launched.

If there is a complicated citizenship case, they can charge more because they are the citizenship experts. Just like you would rather have the most skilled heart surgeon operate on you if you had a heart condition, if citizenship is a migrant's goal, these are the agents they want to work with. This allows us to market these migration agents as the experts in Australian citizenship. And, yes, they do other things like temporary and permanent residencies, but they specialise in the end game – which is citizenship.

So that's an example. It involved a different way of thinking and whole bunch of software systems, but the systems streamlined the business and made it scalable.

So how do you do it? There are three steps:

1. You need to create a product ecosystem.

2. You need to install and use the most efficient technology available.

3. You need to know exactly where you need to drive traffic.

# CREATE A PRODUCT ECOSYSTEM

First thing's first, as usual. Understand exactly whom it is that you're trying to cater to. Over the last few days, I've had a lot of conversations around audience analysis, and I've come across so many different ways that entrepreneurs put it off. They have a very two cents, very weird, very superficial version of who their audience is. If you've skipped a step, please go back to chapter one and go through the questions. Do an exercise around audience analysis. None of this is going to help you if you don't take the time to figure out whom you're talking to and what their problems are.

Now, the product ecosystem is one of the most important things your business can build. When someone thinks that podcasting or blogging or content marketing is what is going to create all their money, that's just not the case. The money comes because of their product ecosystem.

When you start thinking about a product ecosystem, you should do this in three steps:

1.  **DECIPHER** – Break your main service down into effort shared between you and your client.

2.  **EVALUATE** – Figure out the series of steps that your process takes your client through.

3.  **FRAMEWORK** – Draw these steps together into a solution that you can present to your client.

## DECIPHER

The decipher phase is the one where you will probably have to challenge your thinking a lot. Having a few of your peers around you when you do this will really allow you to explore ideas that you wouldn't otherwise. Throughout this phase, you have to ask yourself the most important question of all: What service do you want your business to be known for? If you looked at a dartboard, what would be your business's bullseye?

The concept of the dartboard has been around a while, so I'm not going to take credit for this idea. I do use it a lot though. When you think of providing your ideal service to your ideal client, think of them as being in the centre of the board – the bullseye. If you market to the bullseye, you will have people and services that fall around the edges. This is the idea of niching, which I introduced in chapter one.

When you know what service you would like to be known for, break it up into three options for your client: do-it-yourself, learn-to-do-it and done-for-you. The best way to think of these three variances is in terms of seating on a plane: economy, business and first class. The outcome of getting on a plane is the same; it is how you get there that makes the difference. Another great way to think of this is in terms of how much time your customer has. This could also tell you how much money they have to spend on getting their problem solved.

Depending on the option, as a business, you will need to apply the right amount of time and energy to solving their problem. See the table below:

| | Do-it-yourself | Learn-to-do-it | Done-for-you |
|---|---|---|---|
| Customer Time | 80-100% | 50% | 20-0% |
| Your Business Time | 20-0% | 50% | 80-100% |

With the do-it-yourself option, chances are that the customer is a bit tight on money and has the time to do it themselves given the right instructions. In this scenario, they put in 80-100% of the time. This is the option that gives you the leverage and ability to charge more for the done-for-you and learn-to-do-it options.

If your customer is busy and can't really put too much time into solving the problem they have, but they really want it solved and have the money to pay for it, they will gladly take the done-for-you service, if they trust that you can deliver on what you promise.

Next, we will evaluate how you deliver the solution you promise.


# EVALUATE

The number of times I have met business owners who initially hate me for trying to evaluate their processes is countless. But I guess having written a thesis on quality processes has somehow wired my brain to think in steps. Even this book has multiple steps and frameworks. I challenge you that your business has too. And evaluating what these are is key to your business's growth.

As an example, for someone to go from being a permanent resident in Australia to becoming a citizen, there are five steps. They first need to be introduced to the system, then they need to provide the relevant evidence, followed by filling in the forms, submitting those forms and, finally, knowing what to expect next. Once a resident knows that they are eligible for citizenship, they go through these exact steps.

When it comes to my training program Broadcast Your Message, which teaches clients how to create a podcast, there are seven steps.

These are:

| | |
|---|---|
| **M** | Make clear your concept |
| **E** | Establish your brand |
| **S** | Set up your systems |
| **S** | Structure your recordings |
| **A** | Arrange your recordings |
| **G** | Get on your soapbox |
| **E** | Engage your audience |

Whether the client's approach is do-it-yourself, learn-to-do-it or have it done-for-you, these are the seven steps that I take you through for you to create a podcast that will hit the charts on iTunes.

## RECOMMENDED RESOURCE

To get an exact breakdown of the seven steps to hit the charts on iTunes, go to broadcastyourmessage.com

What are the steps that you take your clients through? How do you solve their problems? Next, think about putting this process into a framework.

# FRAMEWORK

Now that you have evaluated your process, you should put it into a framework. Having a framework gives you credibility. It shows potential clients that you know what the hell you are doing. And rightly so. Just ask yourself the question: How many of my competitors know their framework? How many of them have even taken the time to think about it?

So with Broadcast Your Message, the word MESSAGE encompasses the seven steps of its process in the same way AMPLIFY provides the framework of this book. The bestselling program and book *Become a Key Person of Influence* by Daniel Priestley is centered around 5Ps: Pitch, Publish, Product, Profile and Partnerships. If you work on each of the Ps in the framework, you become a Key Person of Influence. If you follow the seven steps in Broadcast Your Message, you create a great podcast. And if you go through and implement the seven steps in the AMPLIFY framework, you raise your voice, boost your brand and grow your business.

A framework gives you the ability to create collateral around each of the steps in your process and build a course, write a book and even launch an incubator program.

# INSTALL TECHNOLOGY

Now that you have your product ecosystem sorted, you need to identify how you are going to use technology to assist you in delivering your service without you or your staff members being in the room. Or, if you are delivering your service yourself, how to employ technology so you can do it in a one-to-many fashion, like through a webinar or speaking from stage or writing a blog or creating a podcast or a video channel.

Technology has evolved so much that it is managing to replace a lot of what we thought was irreplaceable. I'm pretty sure that there was a time when we thought that traffic police directing cars on the street were irreplaceable. Or that the only way to be heard by millions of people was to go on to a radio show. Or that we had to climb the stairs to get to level six. Nowadays, so much is possible. And when it comes to your ecosystem, here are some of the bits of technology you will require.

# WEBSITE

It is quite amazing that, even today, I meet business owners who don't have websites. Or have websites that are not mobile responsive. Or have no content on their sites. When I say content, I don't mean your 'About Us' page. I mean regular content going up on your website to make your website a living and breathing entity. If your website isn't already on Wordpress, I would suggest fixing that first before you go and do anything else. Not to say that there is no other solution, but Wordpress is the most widely used platform. It has an incredible amount of support and is constantly updated.

# CONTENT

The whole idea of this book is for you to create a content machine that will generate you credibility, leads and lots of search-engine-optimised love from Google. SEO or Search Engine Optimisation is the process that allows a website to be found without paying for advertising. And the only way to do that the right way is to create content consistently.

A very good friend and client of mine, Clarissa Rayward, is a family lawyer. She writes a blog and now has a podcast about law and life at thehappyfamilylawyer.com. Some of the biggest law firms in Brisbane pay Google $54 a click for her name. And this is purely because she has been producing content every week. Why wouldn't you want your business to be found organically?

# PAYMENT GATEWAY

Your website should have a payment gateway. It is not a pathway to hell, even though it might sound like that. It is a way to accept money from your client on your website, and have that money go into your bank account. With Wordpress, there are multiple different ways that you can make that happen, but the most common way is through PayPal. You will need to create a PayPal account and then integrate that with your website, which, for any web developer, is a twenty-minute job. There are other options, like Stripe, but I stick with PayPal because it is so easy to deal with. There is a charge per transaction, so look into that. But with PayPal, you can accept one time payments or recurring payments. Your payment gateway allows you to accept payments without you being in the room. There is no back and forth about bank details and invoice numbers. It is all automated.

## PAYWALL

Per Wikipedia, a paywall is a system that prevents Internet users from accessing webpage content without a paid subscription. And that is exactly what you want. You want your clients to get access to your step-by-step framework after they pay you.

I use a free Wordpress plugin on my website called Paid Memberships Pro. It does the job, enabling me to restrict access to certain webpages and integrate PayPal to accept payment, unlocking access to those pages.

Again, there are multiple different paywall systems you can use, and every one of them has pros and cons. It is important that you pick your paywall software based on what you are trying to achieve. Is it a recurring membership program? Or a one-time online course?

## EMAIL MARKETING SYSTEM

Even though every entrepreneur before me told me how important having an email marketing system was, I ignored it. For the first ten months of the Bond Appetit Podcast, I had no way to capture email or correspond with people that liked my show. Don't do what I did.

The most common email marketing system is MailChimp. You can even get a free account if have under 2000 email subscribers. It is a brilliant option to start off with. You can create a list within MailChimp and put up an opt-in form for visitors to give you their name and email address on your website. If you are on Wordpress, there is a MailChimp plugin that will make your life easy. But collection and storage of email is only the beginning. You will want to communicate with your audience. Start off manually first, then you can create automations to make your life easier.

I started off on MailChimp and have now moved over to ActiveCampaign. With these systems, there is so much you can do.

## RECOMMENDED RESOURCE

For more information about the different types of systems that a business can use to convert leads into clients, check out my friend Justine Coombe's book *Conversion: How to convert prospects into customers.*

Note: You can't add people to your email database without their permission. This is a common habit that is really frowned upon and, if you're doing this from a place of innocence, you should stop making this mistake now.

## PREMIUM RECORDED CONTENT

This content or collateral is what your clients want. Accessing this content is so awesome that they will pay you for the privilege. When you think about premium content, the structure of its delivery is as important as the content itself. Why would someone pay you just for a bunch of good content? I pay if I know that my problem, whatever it is that I'm struggling with, will be solved after I'm done. And I don't want to have to figure out what to do first and where to apply next. I want it all to be in front of me, step by step. When I'm done, I should be a happier person.

You can deliver this content in video form, which is the most common. Or in audio or written word. The video can either encompass you talking to the camera, which was the case with the migration agents, or it could be a bunch of slides and practical screen recordings, as in the case of Broadcast Your Message.

Once you've built your ecosystem, with its technology in place, it is time to breathe life into it.

# DRIVE TRAFFIC

Your ecosystem will remain dormant until you have a living human being that gets injected into it. Sometimes, we get to this stage and feel like most of the effort is done. Then we get slack and rest on the laurels of creating this product. We forget that marketing and driving traffic to it is as important.

When it comes to the migration agents, they create Facebook advertisements that target permanent residents and spend less than $50 per client in ads. That means that they make a net profit of $329 per client. If they can get one client a day for thirty days, that is $9,870 in net profit per month.

Now, the important thing to note is that the ads that your business spends money on should be measureable and specific. You need to know exactly whom you are targeting and how much you are willing to spend on getting a new client.

Once you have a product ecosystem that will produce money without you exchanging your time for it, you can focus on the next three steps of the AMPLIFY framework. The next three steps enable you to create regular content, get people's attention and foster engagement. That engagement is what will get you the trust you need to convert a lead into a client.

For a worksheet to help you create a product ecosystem for your business, go to theamplifybook.com

# CHAPTER 4

# LAUNCH AUDIO

*'Everybody goes through a lot of the same things, and I talk about those, and that's the key. You have to connect with your audience, and I might take them on a trip with me, tell them I went here and I went there and they'll go with me, you know, to hear the stories.'*

**— CHRIS TUCKER**

**NOW YOU HAVE** worked out who your audience is, established your brand identity and evolved a product ecosystem, it's time to get your voice heard. Let me say right from the start, I believe that audio is the best way to reach people. It's the medium where people will consume what you have to offer more regularly.

Everyone's industry has major players whom they would love to be associated with, and there's no better way to connect with them than by being consumable. Because if you're consumable – if your brand is consumable – then people want to be associated with your brand so that theirs gets consumed along with yours.

Let me talk about Dent (dent.global). They've got this amazing personal branding program called Key Person of Influence, which I've actually been through. I've been a client of theirs and now they are a client of ours at Amplify. What Dent do is run these brilliant forty-week incubator programs for entrepreneurs, the result being that they become higher paid, more relevant and more sought after in their business.

Not two weeks ago, I met this guy, Freddie. He came up to me and introduced himself as a financial planner. He said, 'I heard one of the co-founders of Dent speak at an event and I Googled him, and I found his podcast. It's only eleven episodes in. In the last four days, I've consumed all twelve hours of it.' I was just amazed. I asked, 'So how do you know about me?' and he said, 'I found out that your agency produces the Dent podcast and creates all the marketing for them, and so I wanted to chat with you about creating my own.' Brilliant, right? But I said, 'Hold on, before we get into that conversation, how do you feel about Dent the brand right now?' and he replied, 'I love them. It's fantastic. I can't wait for their next forty-week incubator to start.' He was willing right there and then to put money down to join that course. How well does this showcase how much launching an audio program helps people to understand what you stand for and want to be part of it?

When you consider the idea that we can think of something, say it aloud and be heard all around the world, it's incredible. When you think about my podcast Bond Appetit, right now, there's two-thirds of the countries on the planet listening to it. That makes for an exciting concept.

The problem is, the word's a little tainted. Business owners have this idea that podcasting is an activity done by those who have no better work to do. They don't really appreciate what podcasting brings to the table.

Let's look at an example of a similar concept. Back in 2000, Reed Hastings approached the then Blockbuster CEO, John Antioco, and offered him the company he had founded, a company called Netflix, for $50 million. So in 2000, Blockbuster had the opportunity to buy Netflix for $50 million, and do you know what John Antioco, the then CEO of Blockbuster, said? That in his research the numbers did not show that people wanted to sit at home and watch their favourite movies. His research showed that people liked bumping into other people when they went to Blockbuster stores to get the videos that they wanted to watch.

Last year, Netflix surpassed CBS, the television network, and was valued at $32.9 billion. It also reached the $50 million mark in terms of subscribers of its paid service, and has become available in forty different countries (according to CNN Money). Think about how many opportunities get thrown by the wayside because of the way they are expressed and the term that's used to express them.

I need you, as a reader, to think again about the word 'podcasting'. Podcast listeners are loyal, they are engaged, they have disposable income and they are well-educated. Research says that sixty-three per cent of audio listeners buy from the host. They're leaders and they're decision-makers, and they're at the forefront of all the trends. So creating a podcast yourself should be an idea you pay very, very close attention to.

Audio is the only form of content where your audience is allowed to multi-task. They can consume it while they're driving. While they go to the gym. While they mow their lawn. I actually have a listener in a paperless office. She's an accountant and every week, on a Friday, she scans all her paperwork. She likes doing it herself because, apparently, it's very soothing, and while she's doing it, she listens to my podcast.

So, you can do other things while you're consuming the content. When you think about video and blogs and even books, you have to stop what you're doing to consume them. There's no way you can drive and watch a video or read a blog post, but you can listen to whatever you want. And if you subscribe to a podcast, or a piece of audio, it appears on your device – your mobile phone, or your iPod – as soon as the new episode is out. You're not waiting for five o'clock on a Friday afternoon to listen to the content when it's scheduled – you can listen to it whenever you want as many times as you want.

When you realise that, in 2016, all car models come with Apple or Google CarPlay, you start to see what an amazing platform it is for you and your business to be involved in.

Let's take a detailed look at the types of people it works for.

# WHO DOES AUDIO WORK FOR?

It's time to ask yourself whether audio will work for you. Can you picture yourself in any of these scenarios? I'd be surprised if you didn't fit somewhere in this list.

## 1. THOSE WHO HATE TO WRITE

When you're sitting in front of a blank piece of paper or a page in Word or Google Docs, do you find yourself just looking at the screen, not knowing where to start? Does it become so difficult for you that you end up distracted, checking Facebook or something along those lines? If you are in that position, then audio is probably the best tool for you, because it is an easier way to represent all your thoughts and words.

Audio is easier to create because it's easy to talk. We've been talking for ages – it's reading, writing and comprehending that is the hard part. Look at English exams that you take when you immigrate. Because I came from India, Australia made me take these English exams four times, on different occasions, as I went through the whole process of going from being Indian to becoming Australian. And every single time, the speaking component of the English exam was always the easiest. Everyone scored higher on the speaking, because talking is the first thing you learn to do.

It's not only easier to talk, but also easier to get someone else to talk. In business, we're always having conversations. All we need to do is put the right kind of hardware in front of the people whom we're having a conversation with and that's it! That's all we need to do. We don't need to write in a certain way. We don't need to look at a camera in a certain way, and worry about the lighting. We just need to talk.

Audio is also easier to produce than other forms of content. You only have to worry about the audio. The editing, when you produce a blog post or a book, is a lot more difficult. You have to make sure the grammar is correct, the spelling is correct, the punctuation is correct. You have to cut out too much repetition. You can't just have a chat. When you produce audio, all you have got to do is line it up. People like to listen to the way we speak.

## 2. THOSE WHO DON'T ALREADY HAVE EXISTING AUTHENTIC CONTENT

I know a lot of people who pay writers a lot of money to write content for them. I know a lot of people who give writers a bunch of topics and say, 'Go out and write content for us and put it on our blogs, so we get the SEO love from Google, and people find us.' But that's not really the right way to develop content. That's such a mish-mashed way to do it. And Google algorithms are getting smarter – they know when content is created for the sake of creating content. It's a very bad form of content marketing. It's such a waste of time.

You're the one who has the views and opinions about topics in your industry. You're the one who has something to say. You're involved in it. It's the reason why you opened your business. We're talking about education marketing, and if you don't already have an authentic way of creating this content, then audio is your best way of doing it. I guarantee that you have something to say. If you can't find a way to get it out of you, then there are always other people who can do it for you. One of the best ways would be to find a host who can interview you on certain topics.

# 3. THOSE WHO WANT TO DIFFERENTIATE THEMSELVES

Right now, most business owners are trying to be just like their competition. A lot of the time, because we have so much on our plate, all we can think about is trying to beat them by being them, which means we're looking at them as a measuring stick. But if you think about all the memorable brands, they're the ones who have been different and challenged the status quo in one way or another.

There are over 2,000,000 blogs published every single day. And there are about 200,000,000 minutes of video published every single day on YouTube alone. However, there are only about 300,000 podcasts in total at the time of writing this book. There aren't many people doing audio. So, if you're thinking about differentiating yourself – even if your people consume content using other forms, even if you have a great audience when it comes to the written word and video – give them another way to consume your brand. Give them another way to get to know you while they're doing other things.

# 4. THOSE WHO ARE CURIOUS

Have you ever wanted to ask a certain bunch of people questions that you think would really help you move your industry and your thinking forward? When you ask people questions, the answers they give allow you to dig deeper. You can ask them to clarify what they are saying, to build on their response. Have you ever had conversations with people that you just wish were recorded? There are times when, if one of your clients were a fly on the wall, they'd hear such a beautiful conversation that it would push them over the edge and get them to buy from you.

On a podcast, you get to ask these burning questions, and you get to have these great conversations that people can overhear and be part of. When you grow your thinking around the topic, you curate a whole bunch of viewpoints on this one platform and people get to converse about them.

# 5. THOSE WHO WANT TO IMPROVE THEIR SPEAKING AND LISTENING

When you have a podcast, you get regular practise synthesising the thoughts that happen in your brain and making them into words. Outlining what you're trying to say and putting it into words isn't always easy. However, with practise, you get better and better at it. Every single podcaster can go back and say, 'Oh, please don't listen to episode one – it was rubbish.' The reason for that is they got so much better in the way they spoke, in the way they portrayed ideas, in the way they asked questions.

And you, as a business owner, get a chance to evolve the way you speak about your topic, about your business, about your industry. Why wouldn't you give yourself the opportunity to improve your speech by discussing a host of different viewpoints? If, eventually, you're looking to get out there on stage for public speaking engagements and keynote speeches, then there's no better way to prepare than creating audio on a regular basis.

There's also no better way to become a better listener.

A lot of us love talking about ourselves – in fact, it's our favourite topic of conversation. We are absolutely in love with ourselves. And any guest on your podcast is likely to be too. You might find, in general, that you only listen in a conversation to make sure the other person gets to the end of their sentence, so you can make your point and show people how great you are. This means you're a bad listener.

I can't stress enough how important being a good listener is, and if you're wise, it's a trait you want to develop. Really listening to someone else is incredibly powerful. You get to learn more. You get better at understanding what someone else has to say, which means you can have conversations with more substance, digging deeper and asking interesting questions. You get to understand someone else's perspective on a certain topic, which makes you grow as a person. As well as helping you practise speaking, podcasts help you practise listening, so if you want to develop this trait, audio's for you.

# 6. THOSE WHO HATE SELLING

For those who hate selling, audio is probably one of the best tools out there. A sales conversation is usually lopsided – if someone doesn't know you, there's no trust. If you listen to episode 39 of 'Should I Start a Podcast?' at about the 22:30 minute mark, Michelle Falzon talks about these five stages people go through before they start buying from you, before they start trusting you.

A lot of the time, we just create content for content's sake, and I don't think that's the way forward. We need to create content to convert, where conversion doesn't necessarily mean sales, but getting the person to do something, getting them past the point they were at before they consumed this content.

So, if people find out about what you do through the audio you've created, and listen to you, and they develop trust from listening to you, suddenly the sales conversation isn't lopsided anymore. When they want to buy, they ask, 'How long is it going to take for my problem to go away, and when do we start?' It's never: 'How much is this going to cost?' While cost might be a factor, it is not the most important, not where there's already trust.

I used to hate selling, but I've realised over the last few years of putting out audio that my sales conversations are just conversations. You have to realise that conversions happen in conversations – they don't happen when you put out a Tweet on Twitter; they don't happen when you put out an update on Facebook. Through audio, you can have more conversations.

# 7. THOSE WHO WANT TO SAVE TIME

If you're going to have a conversation with someone, why not record it? Based on that conversation, you can create a whole bunch of relevant content, which will not only help your business grow, but also help your business gain trust. If you direct all your potential clients to a conversation that's about thirty minutes long, that's no extra time taken on your part but thirty minutes more that they get to spend with your brand.

If your audio adds value for the potential client, then working with you becomes a no brainer. So if you're in the real estate space, why wouldn't you interview a whole bunch of first-time homeowners who have found a way to hack the system and do things quicker or do things better and create these amazing results for themselves, so that clients in your space can do the same?

# 8. THOSE WHO WANT THEIR PEOPLE TO KNOW THEM BETTER AND CREATE DEEPER ENGAGEMENT

You can share so much through audio, and deliver it in your own authentic voice. Every business owner knows exactly why they started their business. They know exactly what motivated them to put everything on the line, and go through the ups and downs, and no one can explain that better than they themselves. They know what makes them different. So why not share everything you know? If you know whom you're serving, why not create something that you know they will want to listen to?

If you want your people to know you better, audio is the form of marketing for you. It's a way to get people to engage with you and understand what you do, even before they figure out whether you can serve them or not. It's a way for them to hear your real voice. People know that copywriters provide written content – if they can hear your voice and hear you describing something in your own, unique way, then they know it's really you they're listening to. If you really care about your people, you have an opportunity to speak to them directly and invite them to know the real you.

I'll never forget the first time I met Brad Beer, who's an amazing athlete. He's a physiotherapist based on the Gold Coast in Australia, and he met me for the first time at a Key Person of Influence dinner. He shook my hand and he said, 'Hi Ronsley, how are you? How's Rochelle?' It was really weird, because I had never met Brad before. When he saw the expression on my face, he said, 'Oh, I'm so sorry, I listen to all your podcasts when I go for my run, and I feel like I know you, Rons.'

That's not the only time that that's happened, but it was the first time, which is why I remember it so well. The engagement that is created through podcasting is so phenomenal. Your listeners get to know you intimately.

When you have guests on a podcast, the engagement goes both ways. I interviewed my Dad late in 2015, because I wanted to get his story. I've known this man my whole life. We're really close and we have a great relationship. He's my role model; I look up to him for everything, and I chat to him when I come across roadblocks in my life. He's definitely someone who has set the scene for me and how I view life. So I interviewed him, and after that hour-long conversation, I know more about him than I'd known my whole life. There were so many beautiful things that came out that I had never thought about before, never got a chance to ask him. I didn't know that he would love to have dinner with Steffi Graf, for example. He's an entrepreneur who started his own construction company, which he still runs today, but he's also been a sportsman his whole life. I asked him about the similarities between sports and business, and all these beautiful, really amazing bits of conversation emerged that I would never have had a chance to experience if I had not interviewed him.

So trust me, the engagement possible through audio is just second to none.

# 9. THOSE WHO WANT TO GROW RELATIONSHIPS WITH GREATER CONNECTION

When I think about all the guests that I've had on my show, I've interviewed over 200 really successful, awesome people, and they range in terms of what they do, from people with multi-million-dollar companies to people who are just starting off but have had some amazing success. They have all these diverse areas of expertise, from the Director of the Culinary Institute in New York to Pat Flynn, who is known as the small business guinea pig, to people who have written sixteen books to people who have been speakers for years.

I've had such an amazing journey over the last few years interviewing these brilliant people. We've exchanged emails and phone calls and then conversed on the podcast. At the end of an hour, my relationship with them is quite different to when it first started.

Let me give you an example, because I can't stress enough how important these relationships are. When I first started my podcast, I put out a call out to an entrepreneurial group, and I said, 'I've got this podcast and I'm about twenty-five episodes in, and I'd like to interview people around food, and around entrepreneurship.'

There was a doctor, Dr Leandra Brady-Walker, who responded to that call out. I interviewed her the first time and we hit it off. It was a cool interview, so go back and listen to it, if you get a chance, on the Bond Appetit Podcast. But that first interview is not all that happened. It was such a good interview that I ended up interviewing her again. And again. She's now been on my podcast four times. From that point, we became business buddies, and we became accountable to each other. Every two weeks, we would have a conversation about each other's business, and we got really close. It's got to the extent that, a few months ago, when Leandra had her second baby, Eden, Leandra asked me to be Eden's Godfather. I'm very privileged to be a role model in Eden's life. And I promise you, none of that would have been possible if not for the podcast. Audio makes deep connection possible.

Audio is the first sense we develop as children before we are born. That is the reason why we talk to babies in their mother's womb, why we sing to them. There is this genuine connection between sound and the way we feel. There is a brilliant Netflix documentary on how music has changed the lives of elderly people who have Alzheimer's disease, and how audio, not medication, plays such a massive role in them getting back their memories from their childhood. It forms this deep connection between the present and the past, and between people.

Why wouldn't you want to get involved in it? Why wouldn't you, as a business, create this deeper connection? Not only between yourself and your guests, but also with your listeners and your potential clients? Who would you rather buy from: Someone who has sent you ten emails or someone who you've listened to for the last half hour?

# 10. THOSE WHO WANT TO START A MOVEMENT

Every single change in human history can be traced back to a single point where a speech altered the way we saw things. Just think about the big shift in the way we saw race and skin colour, and the 'I have a dream' speech.

We've changed the whole direction of the human race with speeches. And we always have. Someone with a powerful voice and a powerful message can teach us to think differently about something. When Steve Jobs first suggested that they were going to have a phone with only one button, everyone looked at him weird, but now every single smartphone has only one button. And they're trying to make them with no buttons.

There is no better example of starting a movement through a podcast than Serial. It did a lot to move the idea of podcasting forward. In season one, Sarah Koenig, the host of Serial, covered Adnan Syed's murder case, highlighting the fact that there was not enough evidence to prove that he actually killed Hae Min Lee. This podcast created a movement of people who believed in his innocence. Adnan Syed was convicted and got life in prison seventeen years ago, but as of 30 June 2016, he has been granted a new trial. It is fantastic to see the amount of impact that a podcast can have. The fact that someone could get another lease of life, and get to live the remaining part of his life in freedom, is amazing. A podcast can start a movement that allows big changes to happen – it's that powerful.

# LAUNCHING YOUR AUDIO

By now, you should have figured out whether audio is for you. But how do you launch it? There are six steps:

1. Plan
2. Record
3. Edit
4. Produce
5. Store
6. Release

These steps apply whether you want to create a podcast which is a series, or just launch one-off audio segments.

## 1. PLAN YOUR AUDIO

Think about whom you're talking to. Go back, again, and think about what matters to them most. Are they looking for a problem to be solved? Are they looking for a case study? Are they looking for instructions to do certain things? You need to give them that value when you create your audio. So plan.

There's this brilliant quote from Abraham Lincoln, who said that if he had six hours to chop a tree, he would spend the first four of them sharpening the axe. When you go back and figure out exactly whom it is that you're talking to and what matters to them the most, you can use that information to outline what you want to present on your show.

One of the most important aspects to remember with a podcast is that it is a series of audio, all linked together with a common theme. What is the common thread that will link all your episodes together? Why will it be different from anything else out there? And the answer isn't because you will be hosting the show. Please don't be another smarty-pants and just put a bunch of pre-recorded audio that you've collected over the years into a podcast show. Think about your favourite TV show – if there were no story or common thread linking the series together, would you watch the next episode? You want your listener to come back and listen to you again.

Think about the kind of format your audio will take. Will you be doing your audio solo and just talking away? I have an interview-style show, because it allows me to create relationships, and it's easier to talk with someone than talk away on your own. What kind of segments would you have in your show? Could you have a 'Tip of the day'? A review of some sort? Could you have breaking news? Or a quick-answer round in an interview, where you ask three questions really quickly?

If you're conducting an interview, you need to be able to ask your guests questions that really appeal to your audience, and also think of ways that you can get a really good conversation out of them. At the same time, you can plan what to do with that collateral.

Let me give you an example. On my show, the Bond Appetit Podcast, I ask my guests a couple of questions. One question is: 'If you had to choose your last meal on the planet, what would that be?' The other question is: 'If you had the opportunity to share a meal – break bread, have dinner – with anyone on the planet, who would that be?' These are two questions that I repeat in pretty much every single episode. Now what I can do is I can put together an eBook or a PDF of the 'Top 100 meals every entrepreneur wants to eat before they leave the planet', or the 'Top 100 guests who could create the best dinner conversation'. Do you see what I mean? You can create valuable collateral. My audience would love to be able to get a list of the top 100 meals that you should eat before you leave the planet. And it would be a great thing to give away in return for an email address.

So think when you're planning your audio. Think about what's relevant to your audience. Think about creating collateral. And think about whom you're going to talk to, and whether you can find them in your peer group.

It's actually worth having a bunch of questions that I call your 'Go To Questions'. Your Go To Questions are really, really imperative. When you're having a conversation with someone, sometimes the conversation goes astray, and you want to bring it back on topic. You've got to have a few questions that will allow you to do that. You can even go a step further and actually have an entire set structure to your show, asking the same questions of all of your guests, show-in and show-out. EntrepreneurOnFire by John Lee Dumas is a great example. He asks the same questions of every single guest and still creates one of the topmost podcast shows on iTunes.

Here's an example of a few of mine:

- 'What's the best food advice you've ever received?'

- 'What's the most challenging thing that you've ever done as an entrepreneur?'

- 'What is the one cool thing that you'd like to do that you haven't told anyone yet?'

- 'When you think back to your childhood, what is the one memory around food that makes you smile?'

These are my Go-To Questions, just in case I need them.

- How long will your podcast be?

  Think about your people – do they have time to listen to a two-hour podcast?

- Does it make sense to have a ten-minute podcast or would it be better to have a two-minute video instead?

  A podcast should generally be between twenty minutes and forty minutes, in my opinion, because it allows someone to travel to a place and consume that whole episode.

- How often should you release the show?

A lot of people ask me whether a podcast should go out once every month, and I don't necessarily think so. Every week is a good rhythm. The more content you can get out, the better it is for you and the popularity of your show, so think about how often you will release it and why.

Another concept to take into consideration when planning your audio is batching. One of the best things that I've ever been able to do is batch my audio. You can only book an audio interview with me on a Friday, and what ends up happening is that I do four or five interviews every other Friday. This sets me up for the month, and I have enough in the bank that I don't have to worry about creating new episodes every week and finding someone to interview every week.

When you're approaching your interviewees, make sure you've done your research, and prepare them for the show. Some tips include:

- Email them a brief summary of your show and why you'd like to interview them.

- Mention their recent articles, some of their book releases, past interviews and tell them that you'd like to interview them as a result of some of the work that they've done before.

- Keep your messages short and allow them to schedule the

time that works best for them – use something like Calendly or ScheduleOnce, which allows them to make a time in your calendar. This is really, really helpful.

- Tell them the approximate amount of time that you'll need for the interview, and what's going to happen in the interview.

- Let your guests know how the interview will be conducted. Will it happen through Skype, or will it happen in person?

- Tell them what you would prefer they have in terms of equipment (I'll be covering hardware and software in the next step.)

Basically, give them information that will allow them to be as comfortable as possible.

In this planning stage, you should listen to as many different types of podcasts as possible to gain experience of the different audio out there. Then explore your imagination and come up with something new.

# 2. RECORD YOUR AUDIO

Once you've planned your audio, it's time to record. When you're recording, think about the space that you have. Is it appropriate for recording? Is there too much noise? Make sure your microphone levels, and all that kind of stuff, are set up in a way that works for you. Make sure you can listen to your voice as well as your guest's voice when you're recording an interview, because although there's a lot of things that can be done in post-production, the best form of audio comes when it's done properly from the start. Some elements of a bad recording cannot be removed during editing, so pay attention to all the small things. Think about capturing a blurry image as photographer. It is very difficult to fix that image in post production, however good an image editor you are. The same applies to audio.

Let's take a closer look at the hardware and software required in the recording process.

# HARDWARE

These are the pieces of gear you need to record a quality bit of audio:

- Headphones
- XLR Microphone
- 2 to 4 Channel Mixing Desk/ Mixer
- XLR Cable (which will connect your XLR microphone to your mixing desk)
- USB-to-Computer Interface / Adaptor
- 2x RCA-to-RCA Stereo Cables
- 4x RCA-to-6.35mm Mono Adaptors
- Pop Filter
- Laptop

I do understand that this is a bit technical, so for extra help, go to theamplifybook.com. This has a video explaining what everything is and how it fits together, so you can go and watch it and connect everything yourself. There is, however, an easier way to do it: buy a podcasting kit.

## RECOMMENDED RESOURCE

To jump start your podcasting journey, consider buying a podcasting kit. There's a really good podcasting kit called 'Podcast Studio' by Behringer. It's a professional podcast studio bundle with a USB interface that comes in a yellow box with most of this equipment already in there.

## SOFTWARE

When you think about software from an audio perspective, there are two different types you need: Software to set up a line of communication between two parties, and actual recording software.

The best way to set up a line of communication is to use Skype. This is for a variety of reasons. Skype can be downloaded and installed on a Mac or PC and most people already have a Skype address. The thing you need to worry about is connection issues, but it's the same with any phone call – and using Skype is a far better option than recording a mobile phone call. There are also multiple plug-ins available for Skype which will allow you to do a whole bunch of different things.

The second bit of software that you will require is recording software. This is a program that allows your voice to be recorded, then edited and, finally, converted into an MP3 file, which can be uploaded to any media host. Let me give you four options.

The first is ECamm Call Recorder. This is only for Mac. It records Skype calls directly onto your computer. You can choose the quality of the recording, whether you want to record video as well as the audio, and whether you want to record only your guest. You can set it up to record automatically every time you start a Skype call, or use the record and stop buttons. It's a plug-in and all its settings and preferences can be changed through the Skype platform. You can try it for free as well, for seven days.

A version of ECamm Call Recorder that's very similar is called Pamela, and it's only for PC. It's ideally suited for people who want to record a call, a Skype call or an audio-video call on their PC. It has very similar features to ECamm Call Recorder, but in addition, Pamela Call Recorder offers professional functions like note taking, adding notes after you've finished a call, and disabling call recording warnings or sounds during the call.

Audacity is the next option, and available for Mac and PC. It is free and it is next level recording software. You can see the wave forms, and record, edit, add effects, remove noise, import sounds and export sounds. You can record over existing tracks, mix tracks and make the recording seamless – I know a lot of podcasters use this. You can determine and set up sound quality for both input and output, which is really, really valuable. Audacity is good software to play with.

The software I highly recommend is Adobe Audition. I think that it's worth every single cent, and probably the best on the market. The noise removal effects on Adobe Audition are fantastic. It has a really cool template setup. As soon as you set up a template showing the way that you'd like all the audio to appear, whenever you open up Adobe Audition, it'll always appear the same way. Every time I start a new file in Adobe Audition, it's ready to go. Right now it's about $19/ month and it's worth its salt. It is designed to accelerate audio and video production workflows and deliver the highest standards of audio quality. It is by far the best thing that I've invested in when it comes to audio.

I actually use a combination of ECamm Call Recorder and Adobe Audition. With ECamm Call Recorder installed, which means it'll record the Skype call anyway, I also record it on Adobe Audition in case something happens and Adobe Audition crashes (which it never has yet) or, for whatever reason, it doesn't record (which also hasn't happened).

## 3. EDIT YOUR AUDIO

After you've recorded, the next phase is editing. When you come to the editing phase, there are a few tasks involved, but you've got to decide how complicated you want it to be. Do you need to go into the audio and remove all the 'ums' and 'ahs'? Do you need to go into the audio and remove all the sentences that you've started and not completed? When we speak, we do this a lot. We repeat a lot of stuff, say a lot of 'ums' and 'ahs', and 'you know', and we start sentences with 'So'. If you decide to go into your audio and remove all the 'ums' and 'ahs', it becomes more complicated, and is probably worth outsourcing.

You've got to think about what you want to have as part of your audio file. Should you begin with a clip from a previous audio file you have? Should you include a clip of the next audio file? What kind of intro music should you have? What kind of outro music should you have? Should you have a call to action at the end of the audio? Should you have advertisements within the audio? In the editing phase, you take the raw file and make sure that all these little things are part of the ultimate experience when someone is listening to your audio. You take your piece of raw audio and decide what you need to remove from it and what you need to add to it to make sure that it becomes a really good piece of audio content.

# 4. PRODUCE YOUR AUDIO

In the production phase, one of the things that you can and should do is remove background noise. A lot of the time when we record something, noise from other parts of the room gets picked up. Depending on your equipment, you either get a lot of the room being picked up or not much at all. When you record yourself and your guest on separate channels, you can remove background noise separately.

In the editing phase, you've added all these different elements that you need to be part of the ultimate audio, so the next stage in production is to stitch them all together. You should make sure that there's enough of a gap between one audio clip and another, and make sure that it sounds good when it's all put together.

I know that there are podcasts out there that take over twenty-five hours to produce, and even longer, depending on how much information they want included. A lot of the time, it's not necessarily how much information you add but how much information you remove, because you might not need it all. It's about stitching it together correctly and allowing it to ultimately become such a good piece of work that someone says, 'You have to listen to this piece of audio.'

Finally, you need to be able to produce your audio in mono – not in stereo, in mono – with every voice on one channel. There's no point in producing it on two channels. It'll save you a lot of space in the MP3 file that you create and it'll allow it to go across two channels when someone listens to you, as opposed to separate earpieces. When you produce audio, all the channels that you have come together. Production in mono, when it comes to audio, is really, really important, especially when it comes to voices.

# 5. STORE YOUR AUDIO

Here are a few of my tips when it comes to storage. Firstly, you've got to think about keeping all your original files, so have an external hard drive where you store all the original recordings that were on your computer. Audio segments recorded in .wav format are traditionally quite large files. As an example, an hour interview with a guest tends to be about 1GB of storage.

Once you produce the MP3 file, make sure you also have multiple copies of that MP3 file so it's backed up, and make sure you ID3 tag your file. This is really important, because there is no way, right now, for a search engine to go into an MP3 file and find out exactly what's in it. So an ID3 tag stamps your file with the relevant information, so when someone searches for a particular topic, the search engine will go and look at the ID3 tags of all your MP3s and figure out whether they are relevant to the search or not. Meanwhile, if someone ends up downloading the MP3 onto their computer, you want them to know where the MP3 came from. You need there to be a relevant image, and you need there to be relevant tags regarding the artists and where the podcast is from – all the relevant information is stored in the ID3 tag. I can't stress enough how important it is to tag your file.

# 6. RELEASE YOUR AUDIO

Finally, you've got to look at a relevant media host, and find out how it works. Host your audio with someone like SoundCloud, Libsyn or audioBoom. I've used all three of them and I find Libsyn to be one of the best. They do a lot of work within the hosting realm, and they give you really good statistics as to how many people are listening, where they're listening from and what devices they're using to listen to your audio. All these things are relevant, because they allow you to get a better idea of who your people are.

A media host allows you to take the bandwidth of accessing the MP3 file away from your website. If you host the MP3 file on your website, then a couple of things are bound to happen:

1. After a certain number of listeners, your website will crash, which you want to avoid at all costs.

2. You will not know exactly how many listeners you have and where they are listening from.

As a starting point, I suggest getting a Libsyn account and hosting your MP3 files there. It is the most reliable platform for me.

Once you have a media host, you will need to create a feed that you can submit to iTunes or any other radio station. Contrary to popular belief, iTunes doesn't actually store your MP3 files. It only holds a bunch of feed links. You can either submit a feed link directly from your media host, or you can create a podcast feed link from your own website. I use Blubrry PowerPress plugin for Wordpress to create my own podcast feed link. And I use castfeedvalidator.com to validate that I have a feed with MP3 files in it.

So now you know the steps to launching your audio, and all the reasons why you should want to launch audio at all. Starting a podcast may seem like a big step, but if you follow the steps and put the tips into practice, you can unlock all the benefits this form of content brings and have your voice heard by your audience.

Check out the resources at theamplifybook.com for help with the technical aspects of getting your podcast live.

# CHAPTER 5

# INTENSIFY YOUR MESSAGE

*'I'd love to knock an audience cold with one note, but what do you do for the rest of the evening?'*

– ERIC CLAPTON

**ONE OF THE** biggest misunderstandings in marketing is the idea that when you create a message, everyone will flock to your message. That's just not the case. When you create anything – whether it's a blog post, a podcast episode or a video – that's only twenty per cent of the work. Eighty per cent of the work comes from marketing. You need to work to get the attention. Without getting the attention, you can't get the engagement.

Let me tell you how I intensified my marketing for the Bond Appetit Podcast. As soon as an episode got produced, we sent it to Liza. She would take the episode and make notes. Then she would create Tweets, Facebook posts, LinkedIn posts and Instagram images. She would also create a whole bunch of content to help me release an article based on this audio episode. And this was a very low budget operation. Liza's based in the Philippines and it didn't cost me much to employ her to do this. I would get a presence on every single desirable platform, including Pinterest and Slideshare.

So not only did I have this podcast that would go out, but also messaging across all these different social media platforms. It got the attention of people who were on these platforms and took them to the podcast so that they could listen to it and know me better. And that was the primary reason my podcast grew to the extent it did.

For you to achieve the same effect, you just have to create one piece of audio that generates multiple pieces of authentic content that go across a variety of different platforms. And to do that, you need to do two things: identify the platforms that you need to get onto and reverse engineer your audio.

This is the part of the book where things become really cool. You can have so much impact because you've recorded thoughts, ideas and conversations through your audio. This is the part where you take all that beautiful audio and create messages. And those messages are authentic, because they came from you.

So whether you've held an interview, spoken a monologue into a microphone, or captured a bunch of Q and A with a panel – this is where you leverage it. This is where you realise that you've not just created audio for audio's sake.

# LEVERAGING YOUR AUDIO ACROSS MULTIPLE PLATFORMS

Having released your podcast across audio platforms, there are four further platforms that I believe you should pay attention to:

1. **SOCIAL PLATFORMS.** You know that everyone today is available on some social platform or another. We know how much time we each spend on Facebook.

2. **WRITTEN WORD PLATFORMS.** Blogs and articles are probably the original form of content when people think about content marketing.

3. **VIDEO PLATFORMS.** A lot of people will tell you that video is going to explode. Whether you agree or not, it's still an important platform.

4. **RELATIONSHIP PLATFORMS.** You have to find a way to create relationships and maximise those relationships. I think these are platforms that we don't necessarily think of when we first start creating content.

These are the platforms you need to pay attention to in order to intensify your message.

## 1. SOCIAL PLATFORMS

There are so many advantages when it comes to social media. It is by far one of the easiest ways to learn more about your audience. When a business – in any industry – is present on social media and you have a bunch of people engaging with your message, it's very easy to go into the stats and find out, by demographic, exactly who these people are. You can filter your audience by language, by location, and it gives you really in-depth insights. You get to learn more about them. And by interacting with them, you get to know them better. If you've made assumptions at the start regarding who your audience is, this is where you either solidify the assumptions that you've made, or have them challenged and adjust your ideas about them.

So you can intensify your message by targeting your audience more effectively. If you know who your people are, you can go into your social media platforms and target them by location, language, age, gender, relationship status, education … There are so many different ways to talk to your audience. Social media helps your customers share your information with other people who could potentially be your customers, and all of a sudden your audience has grown. You instantly get new leads. You're not even selling to people – you're just coming to their attention at the right point in their lifecycle.

Social media also allows you to get instant feedback. As soon as you put stuff out there, you get instant commentary on your customers' perspectives. When you launch a new product and you share it on social media, you instantly know what your people think of it, and whether they think it's a great idea or a bad idea, and if there's something you've missed. It is so powerful to get instant feedback. The last thing that you want to do is spend all this money on launching a product that your people don't want.

Social media gets you ahead of your competitors. A lot of your competitors don't know that they should be present in these places. They don't know the advantages of being present in these places, or how to access the relevant information. If you're the one who can solve your customers' problems and you're the one actually giving them that message, they will obviously come to you and buy from you.

Increasing your traffic and improving your search ranking are among the biggest advantages of social media. But where should you be? Let's look at some of the platforms more closely.

I've already mentioned how much time we spend on Facebook. We wake up in the middle of the night looking at our Facebook feed. The amount of time we spend on Facebook is actually really interesting. There's this new app I have installed on my phone and it tells me exactly how much time I spend there, and it is ridiculous (it's enough to get me off Facebook for a few days just to restore some sanity!). Being present on Facebook is a no brainer because of the amount of people already present on it.

Twitter has been around for ages and one of its biggest perks is the ability to search – you can get really cool results on twitter.com/search. Imagine you're a mattress company. If that's your business, then how great is it that you can go and find people already talking about their problems? Type in: 'I really need a new mattress,' or 'I had a really bad sleep,' or 'My insomnia is acting up again.' Twitter is probably the best way to find people who need you. Obviously, you need to have some content on there as well. Look up Gary Vaynerchuk, who uses Twitter to great success. The main thing to note is that Twitter is a platform that you have to be present on. Followers are not as important as the ability to engage with people.

Next, let's think about Instagram. It's probably one of the fastest growing social media platforms out there. There's so much hype around Instagram and it being bought by Facebook. When you think about the people who actually engage on Instagram, and grow their following, it's primarily because people actually like what they see. It's all about visual stuff. Being present on Instagram is important because there are ways that businesses can use it to achieve some great marketing goals. When someone gets onto your Instagram profile, they can scroll through a wide variety of different images. It creates this collage that gives a customer an idea of what you're really about. So if you have a really cool balance of fun and business images, it tells people a lot about what kind of business you are. For example, you could have a balance of business images and images around inspirational quotes – that's what we have on We Are Podcast.

Instagram allows you to have a very visual representation of your business, and you can also create engagement with contests, getting your Instagram followers to share things about your business and post images for you. Everyone has a phone in their pocket, and if they add a hashtag of your business name and it starts trending, your reach grows and your message is intensified. People also go onto Instagram and search for different hashtags, so if you're that mattress company and you search '#insomnia', you'll find your people. So think about Instagram in terms of how you can reach the audience that you want to reach. That's why knowing who your audience is is so important. If you have events, you can get attendees to hashtag and share their different images, posting to Facebook and Twitter at the same time. So if you have fifty people capture an image during your event, you have fifty different perspectives going out on all these platforms, easily searchable because of the hashtag.

Meanwhile, Pinterest is very popular amongst women and also very visual. There are massive shops that use Pinterest for their marketing. The biggest pull of Pinterest is that it gives you SEO love, which other forms of social media don't do as powerfully. So even having a token, short-term presence on Pinterest is beneficial.

A lot of people will tell you that Google+ is not trendy anymore, and that you don't need to be present there, but it is brilliant for your search engine ranking. If you have your messages shared on Google+, when someone searches for terms you've tagged, you'll come up high in the search results. So you get better traction, even if it's just a simple message and you don't engage with your audience on that platform.

A lot of professionals and B2B customers are present on LinkedIn. It allows you to get your message out to people who have their own LinkedIn profiles. Considering that they were just bought by Microsoft, LinkedIn are definitely looking for ways to get more people to come to and stay on their platform. So having your personal LinkedIn profile up and running is important.

These are the key players to pay attention to when it comes to using social platforms to intensify your message. I'll talk about how to reverse engineer your audio in order to share your message to best effect once I've run through the other platforms.

# 2. WRITTEN WORD PLATFORMS

Articles and blogs were the first form of content marketing, and there are massive, massive benefits to being present in written word format. I believe that every business needs to publish at least one article a week. I'm going to give you a few of the advantages of intensifying your message through the written word.

Let's start with the ability to increase search engine traffic. We want to be able to pull people towards us when they are looking for a business or looking for solutions for their problems. Rather than saying to people, 'Come buy from me. Buy from me. Buy from me,' you'd rather say to people, 'Well, are you facing this particular problem? Are you not sleeping at night? It could be that you have a bad mattress.' If you have written word content, reasons to come to you will come up when they're searching for the problems that they wish to solve, and the chances of them buying from you are quite high.

You basically increase the long-tail search results for certain terms. Let me give you an example. 'How do I get a good night's sleep five out of the seven nights of the week?' is a long-tail search phrase. If someone looks that up, then having relevant content on your website allows you to rank higher, which is valuable because these kinds of key phrases lead to high conversions. When someone searches something like that, the top results are usually the ones that they love to look at.

Having written content on your website portrays you as an expert in your field to the search engines. And this is what really improves conversion rates. According to Hubspot (hubspot.com), an overall return on investment is more likely for businesses who have a blog. They go as far as to put a number to it: There's thirteen times the return on investment year after year for businesses who prioritise a blog as an experience when someone comes to their website.

Your content also allows you to generate inbound links. An inbound link means someone linking to your website or to your article in their own content. Having written content available to authors, columnists, journalists, bloggers and contributors means they have something to cite, and the link raises the profile of your site. That's very, very powerful.

The more content you have the better. Hubspot does a lot of research around inbound leads and inbound marketing, and according to them, businesses with between 400 and 1000 pages of content get six times the leads than those with 51 to 100 pages of content. Don't let the numbers scare you – the most important thing that you need to remember is that the more content you have on your site, the more leads you get.

Meanwhile, having a blog on your website will support your social media initiatives. And if you have a blog post that complements your audio content, it tends to give people a chance to come back after listening. If you think about having four podcast episodes in a month and then sending a monthly newsletter out to your people, you could summarise those four episodes, instead of creating new content every time you want to create a newsletter. Or, say twenty episodes down the line, you could create all this blog content around your episodes and pull that together into a really nice giveaway, allowing people to opt in and give you their email addresses.

You can also leverage your written word content across other people's platforms, which will drive traffic back to your website. You can appear on the websites of your peers with guest blog posts, and you can approach a bunch of businesses who curate content. They have a huge amount of guest bloggers who post on their website. I write for Flying Solo, Smallville and Key Person of Influence, and it does drive traffic back to my website because of the content I put out there. Lots of people go to these high-conversion sites.

LinkedIn Pulse is another great option for putting written word out there. It allows your professional connections on LinkedIn to view the posts you write, which raises your credibility on LinkedIn. Another platform owned by LinkedIn is called SlideShare. It basically allows you to post a bunch of slides, and there is a lot of traffic. A lot of people go onto SlideShare to look at the new and different slides posted up there. This also serves to drive traffic to your website, along with bigger platforms like Medium, Quora and Reddit.

In summary, written word platforms offer a huge space to leverage to intensify your message.

# 3. VIDEO PLATFORMS

In recent history, there has been no shortage of information telling us how great video is. Video allows us to use different senses, both sight and sound. You get a perception of who the person on camera is, though that also means you make a lot of judgements, even before they actually open their mouth. There are a variety of issues with video, including how complicated the creation process is and how complicated the editing process is. However, it has become easier over time to allow for those complications – video still requires more work than blogging and audio podcasting, however, you need to be present on video as a business, and I'll give you few reasons why I think that's the case.

The SEO factor is massive. The dominance of social media as a marketing tool has grown exponentially, and the ability to give someone a quick two-minute video demonstration of your services instead of them reading a long text version is awesome. Getting to see exactly who you are increases trust.

YouTube search results get ranked really highly. YouTube is one of the largest search engines in the world after Google, so you need to have a presence there. Video also allows you to take advantage of great distribution mechanisms – there are several video distribution sites that allow you to upload your video. When you think about the different video sharing sites, like YouTube, Dailymotion, Vimeo and Facebook, it's quite easy to upload the same video to all these places, and get a lot of attention. Facebook has become massive in terms of allowing your video to be seen by more of your people. One of the biggest complaints about Facebook over the last few years has been that the posts that we put up on Facebook are not seen by all our followers, all our friends or all our fans. However, when it comes to video, the percentage of people who actually see our content is really high.

Finding different ways to publicise video is also an interesting area. Facebook has their own Facebook Live platform and Twitter has bought over the likes of Periscope, which is live video streaming. Meerkat is another early player in the game. Live video streaming is a huge way to get to the people who actually care about what you have to say. I remember I once did a Periscope interview of someone who had a cake business and I had about 120 live viewers from all over the planet. It's a massive platform that enables you to get yourself seen by people who don't even know that you exist, and intensify your message.

It automatically increases the brand value of your website if you have video, audio and text on it. If you have a really well done video on your 'About Us' page, it increases the time someone will spend on your website. Andrew Griffiths quite often tells the story of how he gets a lot of enquiries from people who have been on his website and seen videos of him speaking on stage. They don't even ask him how much his speaker fees are. They ask, 'Can I have this topic, this topic and this topic put together and can you create us a new presentation based on these topics? We love what we hear. We love the videos that are on your website. We don't need to see any more.' If they like it enough, people will actually stop what they're doing and actively engage with your brand. And if anyone has doubts around certain aspects of your offering, a video does help increase sales. It allows for better opt in and better subscriber lists if you're looking to get people onto your email list. So being present on video is a massive advantage.

# 4. RELATIONSHIP PLATFORMS

Relationship platforms don't immediately come to mind for some reason, however, they're probably the most powerful platforms of all, so I'm going to talk about them and give you an opportunity to think about how you can use them to intensify your message.

When you interview someone, your guest becomes a relationship, and when you have that relationship, they become your ally. Once you have allies, you can work with them in ways that both grow your business and help them grow their profile as well. Doing little things like sending them an email to let them know that their episode has gone live and where they can share it, or even giving them an image to share, is good practice. It's actually one that I wish I applied more from the very beginning. If you have a page where you list all your guests and their websites, it allows your guests to be seen, and the likelihood of them reciprocating is quite high. This ties into the link factor that I spoke about in the written words section.

Another way of making allies is to create mastermind groups. These allow you to share challenges, business ideas, different perspectives, and cross-promote products across each other's different platforms. Both Facebook and Google have different ways in which you can create groups and communities. These are all relationship platforms. The trick is to make a valuable contribution to these groups and communities. They all come together to increase the quantity and quality of relationships that you have, extending your reach and helping your business function.

When you make people your allies, it deepens your connection and it allows you to create partnerships. So if you have an ally with a similar audience and no competitive overlap with you, you can create a brilliant partnership with them. If your product or service is in alignment with their product or service, you can combine the two and give both your people and their people a really good deal on both your services, increasing the value that you give them. Then, when it comes to your partner, you can share their content and they can share yours, thus intensifying your message. So partnerships are huge. If you're not thinking of partnerships right now, I guarantee that's lots of money that you're leaving on the table. The main thing to realise is that in order to create a partnership, you need to have established a relationship. You can't just rock up to someone and say, 'Hey, let's have a partnership. Give me some of your people.' Just like when it comes to your people, you need to develop trust. And it's imperative that your values align. The last thing you want is to be stuck in a partnership with someone whose values do not align with yours. At least one of you ends up looking really bad.

So think about making allies, forming groups and forging partnerships – these are your relationship platforms.

# HOW TO REVERSE ENGINEER YOUR AUDIO

I know what you must be thinking. You must be thinking, 'Ronsley, it's great that you're telling me all these platforms are valuable, why they're valuable and that I should be present as a business on all of them. But how do I make this happen? I don't have the time!' I see what you're saying. But it is possible and it doesn't have to take up too much time. I'm going to give you a framework, a recipe, a way to make it happen on the back of the audio that you recorded in the last chapter.

Whether you've interviewed someone, someone's interviewed you, or you've just captured a monologue, this is what you need to do next: Reverse engineer the audio that you've created. What do I mean by reverse engineering? You need to collect a bunch of information from the audio that you've created. I'm going to give you a framework so you understand exactly what I'm trying to say.

And I'm going use episode 35 of Should I Start A Podcast to help illustrate some of the information I'm trying to extract.

## RECOMMENDED RESOURCE

Listen to episode 35 of Should I Start A Podcast at wearepodcast. com/035

First, listen to the audio and collect the following bits of information:

- Take out three things that make you or your guest famous. If you're talking to someone, get their bio. You want the information that means when someone reads it, they think, 'This person is credible and I need to start listening to this person. They have something to say based upon the problems I need to solve.' For example, in episode 35 of Should I Start A Podcast, I spoke with Omar and Nicole, who are the creators of the $100 MBA show. The three things that we pulled from this conversation were:

  - Omar has fourteen years of business building experience.

  - Nicole is a New York Film Academy graduate.

  - The $100 MBA gets over 50,000 listeners per day.

- Write down ten things that were spoken about. What are the top ten subjects covered? Going back to episode 35 and the example above, these are the top ten subjects we covered with Nicole and Omar:

  - The $100 MBA podcast and how they make it happen seven times a week.

- How they recorded, edited and produced their first 300 episodes by themselves.

- The difficulty in doing a daily show in terms of quality, content and consistency.

- The reasons behind their success.

- The fundamentals of business – the whole purpose of the $100 MBA show.

- How podcasting has changed their business.

- The launching of the $100 MBA online training and community.

- How podcasting can build long-term relationships.

- The importance of competitions in order to have a sustainable program.

- The money aspect of podcasting.

- Now write a top ten list of takeaways. What are the biggest 'Ah-HA' moments? What are the biggest lessons you can take from the conversation or monologue? With Nicole and Omar, we created this list:

  - When starting out with your podcast, it's important to involve yourself with all areas of the show's production.

  - Always be careful to adjust your show as you grow.

  - Your show always wants to be growing.

  - Don't be afraid to experiment with new ideas.

  - Earn your audience's trust by being entertaining and consistent with your content and output.

- Once you have a popular, growing show, you can begin thinking about monetising it.

- It's important to podcast at least once a week.

- It's important to be original with your content and the structure of your show.

- Ask yourself how your podcast is different.

- Make sure that any sponsors will appeal to your audience and fit in with your show's ethos.

- What are the top six quotes? These can be from you or the guest – what soundbites are worth making note of? Here are three quotes that we pulled from Omar and Nicole's episode:

  - 'I think if you're just getting started with your podcast, you should do everything yourself. You have to understand the inner workings of every aspect of the podcast.'

  - 'We have adjusted the show as we grow. We've made some changes, added some content; we've changed different themes of the show. We experimented a lot. Sometimes things work and things don't.'

  - 'You can't sell to nobody. You have to grow an audience. You have to have somebody to speak to, and that should be your main focus when you start building your podcast.'

- What are the three top action items you want someone listening to this audio to do at the end of it? It could be going and reading a book. It could be as simple as going and checking out a website. It could be going and downloading a bunch of videos. The action items are important. Here are some actions that we think a listener should take as a result of listening to episode 35 of Should I Start A Podcast:

- If you're not getting the number of listeners you'd like for your show, ask yourself what you're missing and consider restructuring your podcast.

- Write down a list of three practical and actionable steps you could take to improve your podcast's visibility.

- Are you consistent with the amount you podcast? If not, consider why and how you can change that. Perhaps you need to bring in external help.

- What are three key resources mentioned in the audio? This is self-explanatory – what resources have you directed your listeners' attention to, whether it's websites, books and/or videos?

So, at the end of this process, you have six bits of valuable content. Now this is the cool part. When you have all this information, do the following:

1. Take the top three action items and create three Facebook updates around them. Allow your team or a graphic designer to create an image that highlights the audio you've created. You can release one of these every week for the next three weeks. If you have a weekly show, then every week, you can tell your audience that there is a new audio episode out, but also that there are previous episodes that they could've missed. I wouldn't release more than three Facebook updates a week.

2. Take the top ten takeaways and three of the six top quotes, put them together and create thirteen Tweets that drive traffic to that piece of audio. Because the life of a tweet is

so short, you can release a tweet every one to two hours through a scheduling program like Hootsuite, or Buffer.

3. Then take all six quotes and make six Instagram images out of them. Canva (canva.com) is a great program to use for this. It's online image creation software that lets you produce images that cater to a whole host of different platforms.

4. Now create three Pinterest images, or use three of the same images you created previously for Instagram. You can create them around three of the quotes or around the action items.

5. Next, take the six bits of content that you've created and put them together into a slide deck that you can upload to SlideShare. The more slides you create with smaller pieces of bite-sized information, the better for SlideShare.

6. Create a brief live-stream video to announce the top ten subjects covered in your audio. If live video scares the bejesus out of you, then use the slide deck you've created in step 5, and create a screencast with you talking to each of the slides. Make your video less than four minutes and upload it to YouTube, even to Facebook if you wish.

7. The last step is the written word. Create a blog post out of the six bits of content to complement your audio. If you can, get an ally to share the article on their platform; you get the advantage of reaching their audience too.

Within all this, if you have an interview type show, and you haven't emailed and kept in touch with the guests that have been on your show, then, as a business owner, you are shooting yourself in the foot. Relationships are key to any business functioning and the more you foster them, the quicker you are going to succeed.

So now you have a variety of content leading to your audio that can be present on LinkedIn Pulse, Medium, Tumblr, Twitter, Pinterest, SlideShare, Facebook, Instagram, YouTube … every platform you please.

Now, if you do want a graphic designer and a content writer and a social media expert to get your message out in all these different forms, you can outsource this step. You've got your audio, so you have this authentic content which is yours. This means getting it out on your platforms can be delegated to someone who understands your business and shares your values. That's what we do at Amplify – we actually do that for you. We have a whole marketing team that plugs into this and we do this week in, week out, day in, day out. We help businesses be present on all different platforms.

Regardless, when this great content, born of your audio, is present on all these different platforms, you get attention. You're leveraging your audio, already present on your chosen audio platforms, and intensifying your message across your social platforms, your written word platforms, your video platforms and your relationship platforms. You're grabbing people's attention on all these platforms. The next step is to turn that attention into engagement.

For a worksheet to help you intensify your message, go to theamplifybook.com

# CHAPTER 6

# FOSTER ENGAGEMENT

*'A good teacher, like a good entertainer first must hold his audience's attention, then he can teach his lesson. '*

— JOHN HENRIK CLARKE

**AS SETH GODIN** says, 'We are leaving the industrial economy and entering the connection economy.'

There has been a genuine shift in the way business operates today. And there has been a genuine shift in exactly what we want as people. In the industrial age, we focused purely on efficiency. We focused on getting people to do the same thing over and over again, and to get good at those jobs. But, now, we want connection.

Getting potential clients' attention is not the end of the marketing process. In fact, it's just the beginning. You need to go on to get engagement and get them to spend time with you. You want to connect with them. You want to form a relationship with them.

One of the biggest issues that we face as business owners is that potential customers don't spend enough time with our brand to really understand what it is that we do and why we do what we do. And we struggle to prove credibility and we struggle to prove that our solutions will help them.

There's a really important concept called Zero Moment of Truth (ZMOT), which came from a study done by Google. The crux of the study is that potential clients need to come into contact with about eleven touchpoints, or spend seven hours with you over four different platforms (podcast, social, blog, e-book, etc.) before they're ready to buy from you.

So in this particular step, what we're trying to do is bring potential customers to that Zero Moment of Truth. You want to get them to the stage where they already know how good you are and what you do and why you do what you do. Now all they want to know is how to buy from you. You've built trust through engagement.

Let me talk to you about Jesse Green. He's a dentist who specialises in mentoring dentists with their own practices. What tends to happen, in his opinion, is that dentists are great at what they do – they're fantastic dentists – but they're not great business owners. So he teaches dentists the business skills they need to run successful dental practices. Jesse joined us as a client about 1.5 years ago and he created his own podcast called the Savvy Dentist.

I spoke with him a couple of weeks ago and he said to me that, as a result of the Savvy Dentist, he doesn't have capacity to take any more clients on, because he's fully booked. It only took eight episodes for him to be at capacity, which is such an amazing result from a podcast. He interviews a whole bunch of different people who have done some amazing work within the business realm, and he aligns that with dentists, and he gives them something to do. He gives them a way to look at their dental practice from a business standpoint, which no one else is doing out there. Jesse told me that he can directly attribute $80,000 in revenue to the first twelve episodes of his podcast.

Jesse has got amazing results from creating engagement through his podcast. The important things that Jesse established to get to that increase in revenue include the following:

- He worked out who his audience is, what makes him different and who his peers are (the guests on his show).

- He spent a lot of time and money on moulding his brand. Visit drjessegreen.com; you will notice that all the elements he puts out there are consistent with his brand.

- He created a product ecosystem and has a product where he trains and coaches dentists to create better businesses.

- He launched his audio, which is the Savvy Dentist Show.

- He uses social media and blog posts to drive traffic to his podcast, which allows potential leads to engage with his brand for hours on end.

In chapter four, we spoke about how to create authentic content through audio and why that's so powerful. Then, in the last chapter, I detailed how to make sure that authentic content gets broadcast across social platforms, written word platforms, video platforms and relationship platforms, and how you use that to get attention.

Attention is where people stop and notice you, right? But the key is engagement. It takes engagement for people to get to know you and get to like you. When they like you, that's when they begin to trust you, and then selling to them becomes an easy proposition. You want to keep people listening and keep them coming back until you reach the ZMOT. This is so much easier if you have audio, because your listeners get to spend more time with you.

Think about the average Tweet – the average Tweet is 140 characters, which is really short. It doesn't live very long – less than a few seconds, because it quickly gets lost in the noise. Meanwhile, your average blog post is between 500 and 1500 words, which takes about seven minutes to read. The average YouTube video is four minutes and twenty seconds. In contrast, the average length of a podcast is between thirty-five and forty-six minutes. Mine is an hour. So if someone starts listening to your series, that becomes a lot of time you spend together.

But engagement isn't just about listening to you and being exposed to you. Engagement is as much about audience participation as it is about what you have to say. The end goal is not that they merely listen. The end goal is that they take action after listening. They're more likely to do this if they've gotten involved in your discourse.

# ENGAGING YOUR AUDIENCE

Here are a few things you can do to increase audience participation:

## 1. ISSUE CALLS TO ACTION

What exactly is it that you want your audience to do after listening to your show? Once they get to like you? Do you want them to subscribe to an email newsletter? If they subscribe to an email newsletter, then you can communicate with them differently there. Do you want them to listen to another episode? Do you want them to review and rate you? If you leverage your reviews and ratings on iTunes and any other platform that you have, then you can increase your reach.

My show Bond Appetit was on top of iTunes in the banner section for over five months, next to ABC Radio and Triple J. This was a very powerful position to be in, but what I didn't do was leverage it. Early on, I did not issue any calls to action. The difference when I started to do this was massive in terms of engagement, in terms of getting my audience to participate in what I was doing.

From the very beginning, we need to be able to train the listener to take an action, whatever that action might be. It might be to sign up for a course. Or go and read an article. Or download something. Or share what they've heard with their friends. We want to prompt them to engage with our message in some form. We want to prompt them to act in a way that benefits them and benefits us.

# 2. ENCOURAGE DIALOGUE

You've always got to think about your ideal listener, the person that you're trying to talk to. Whether you're interviewing someone on your podcast or addressing the listener directly, every time there's a new concept mentioned or a term that has multiple definitions, clarify it for your audience, but don't just talk at them. Ask your audience a question through the conversation. Give them a chance to think – allow them to ponder the subject you're talking about or the conversation that you're having with your guest.

You're providing value to your people, but you're also getting them to think, compelling them to form their own questions. So make sure that there is a way that they can contact you – so that you can actually enter into a dialogue with them.

There's a really cool app called Speakpipe which you can install on your website and someone can leave you a voicemail there. Whether you use this or just a function where someone can comment on what you put up, the important thing is to make sure that there is a feedback loop for someone listening so they can come and leave information for you. This means you also hear what they have to say and can talk back to them, making your interaction an exchange.

Make sure you invite them to contact you on your website or on Facebook or on Twitter. And make sure you actually engage with them there. Don't just schedule your posts leading people to your audio and then leave them there to gather likes and comments. Talk back to your audience and invite them to participate in the conversation. Engage them in discourse.

## 3. SET QUICK-WIN QUIZZES

You need to nurture your audience. You wouldn't go up to someone whom you've never met before at a bar and say, 'Let's get married.' That's just not how it works. You need to engage with them first. You need to develop a relationship.

You've introduced yourself to your listeners and you've got their attention. Now you've got to go on a series of dates. You want to provide them with something of value and entertain them. You want them to give you their number, their email address, and keep coming back for more. A good way to kick this off is to talk about mistakes. Often, a first date involves a lot of comparing dating stories – or war stories. And that comes back to the mistakes people make when they've got a problem to solve. Helping them identify their mistakes gives them a quick win. It's a success they want to share.

So how can you get people to identify the mistakes that they're making? A checklist is a great idea. It gets them on the road to fixing their problem, just by going through a bunch of steps that tells them exactly what they need to do. If they realise they're missing a step on the checklist, in their head, they feel like it's a quick win.

Quizzes are another great way to do the same thing. If you have a questionnaire that you take your people through which gives them a result they can grade on a scale, they are more likely to share it with other people.

Think of the success of all the quizzes around. You see it on Facebook a lot, when people identify with a character on their favourite TV show, or those quizzes that allow them to categorise their personality, putting themselves in a box. It's quite interesting, but people like to share the results. It's the same when you go on a really good date – you tell all your friends.

So these are the keys to gaining audience participation and fostering engagement. You keep providing value to your audience and you keep inviting them to take action and you keep encouraging dialogue between you and you invite them to celebrate quick wins.

They come to like you and they learn to trust you. Before you know it, you're at the final stage in the relationship, the sales stage, where you commit to each other – you're engaged.

For a worksheet to help you foster engagement, go to theamplifybook.com

# CHAPTER 7

# YIELD ON INVESTMENT

*'Every time we make an investment decision at FedEx, we*
*ask ourselves: "What is the return on this investment?"'*

— FREDERICK W. SMITH

**AS SOMEONE KNOWN** in quite a few circles as 'The Podcast Guy', I get this question a lot: 'Ronsley, your podcast is great, but how do you make your money?' And it keeps coming back to where I *spend* my money. It keeps coming back to being able to measure what I'm doing so I'm never naive when it comes to my marketing escapades. If you spend money on a certain marketing strategy and you don't know how much revenue you brought into your business as a result of spending that money, then you have a problem. If you're not sure what kind of metrics you need to measure, and you end up measuring nothing, you have a problem.

As a business owner, when you spend money, you want to make sure that you get a return on investment. You want to know exactly how much a $100 spend on a particular activity will bring you back in revenue. If you know that you spent $100 on an activity and it brought you back $10 in revenue, then you know there's no point continuing this process. You need to know how to measure the return you yield on your investment so you can improve upon it. So you need to be measurable.

Now, there's no better way to be measurable than to have a podcast because, let me tell you, numbers and statistics come from everywhere. I want to talk about the WTF Podcast. It's a podcast that is pretty famous – they get over 325,000 downloads per episode. Marc Maron, the comedian who's the host of the show, even had President Obama on his podcast. They very confidently tell their advertisers, 'Every single time you advertise with us on one episode, we can guarantee that 325,000 people are going to listen to your message.' And if you think about how much people charge in terms of advertising, that's about $8,000 per episode spot on average. If you do four episodes a month, man, that's a lot of money. But it's worth it from the advertisers' point of view when you think about the results of this survey that has been done by Midroll. They did a survey of about 300,000 podcast listeners, and they found out this key statistic: Sixty-three per cent of those listeners had bought something that the host of the show they tuned into promoted.

Meanwhile, going back to the WTF Podcast, about ten percent of their listeners – that's about 35,000 to 36,000 people – pay between $1.99 and $8.99 for basic or premium membership. That's a minimum of $70,000 just from ten percent of the listeners.

Now, those statistics are important because they're being measured. They mean that the show knows where its revenue is coming from and, therefore, where they should invest. For you to do that, you need to implement a measuring and improvement strategy.

Success is key, and to know if you're successful, you need to measure what success looks like. We can get sucked into this vortex of doing tasks. We invest time, money and energy into nice-to-do activities that make us feel like we're busy. However, at the end of the day, we really need to understand that they're just activities – they don't really contribute to whatever goal we're trying to achieve. When we implement any new strategy – whether it's a marketing strategy, whether it's an innovation strategy, whether it's a new email service even – we need to find out whether it falls into this black hole of just being an 'activity' or whether it's contributing to the greater good of our business. Do you know what it is that you'd like to achieve when it comes to your business? Because looking at it from that point of view makes measurement a lot easier. So if you haven't done it as part of step one, go back and figure out at least three goals that you want your business to achieve. Where is it that you want to be in the next year, in the next three years, in the next five years?

There's no better example than Tesla. On 2 August 2006, Elon Musk wrote a blog post on the tesla.com website. He introduced himself and he gave a background of exactly what he does. He said, 'My day job is running a space transportation company called "Space X", but on the side I'm the Chairman of Tesla Motors.'

He then outlined this plan. His plan over the next ten years was to achieve four things:

1. He wanted to create a low-volume car. This would be an expensive car.

2. He would use the money from the people who bought that car to develop a medium-volume car at a lower price.

3. He would use the money from the people who bought those two models to create an affordable high-volume car.

4. He would provide solar power for everyone.

And he's achieved that. He's then taken that plan from 20 July 2016, and roughly ten years later (give or take a few weeks), he's come up with the master plan for the next ten years.

This is what he has outlined as his master plan for the next ten years – again, there are four big goals that Tesla Motors wants to achieve:

1. Create stunning solar roofs with seamlessly integrated battery storage.

2. Expand their electric vehicle product line to address all major segments.

3. Develop a self-driving capability that is 10x safer than manual via massive fleet learning.

4. Enable your car to make money for you while you aren't using it.

Now, when you think about a lot of the big companies who have achieved brilliant success in their business lifecycles, they have only done that because of the goals that they have set. So goals and visions are super important. They bring together your people, your clients, your suppliers – everyone involved with your business – enabling them to focus on what the most important thing is to your business. This helps you make easier decisions, especially when it comes to measurement.

So, on the way to our goals, we want to know whether we're spending our money wisely. Whether we're spending our effort wisely. Most importantly, whether we're spending our time wisely. But how do we know?

# METRICS

I believe that there are three main metrics that you need to look at in order to properly measure the return you're yielding on your investment. These are:

1. Trust metrics

2. Relationship metrics

3. Analysis metrics

These sets of metrics allow you to measure your strength in different areas to form an overall idea about how well your marketing and your business are performing.

# 1. TRUST METRICS

It's always been the case that people buy from businesses and brands that they know, like and trust. Trust is how you go from getting attention and getting engagement to getting sales. Someone's not going to buy from you unless they trust that your product is going to solve a problem that they have. If you're not measuring trust metrics, then I think you are missing a trick.

Here are the trust metrics that you need to consider:

# I. TOTAL SHARES

When it comes to social media and any content that you put out there, why are shares important? It's because people only share your content and recommend that others read it or listen to it if they identify with the message. They won't share if they don't identify with the message. If they don't believe in what you're trying to achieve. If they don't think that what you're saying makes sense.

Let me give you an example. For the last three years, whenever I've been to a restaurant, I've never ordered off the menu. I sit in the restaurant, don't look at the menu and I always ask the waitstaff what they recommend. It doesn't matter whether it's a mum-and-dad restaurant or a fancy restaurant, even a takeaway. I always ask what they recommend and I always pick that dish. I have not, in the last three years, ever been disappointed with whatever suggestion has been made to me by the restaurant. And I'll tell you why that is. Someone is not going to recommend you something if they don't believe that you will be satisfied by it, because they have to face you once you've consumed it. Even a friend is not going to recommend your business or your services to another friend if they don't believe that you can deliver on your promise (whatever that promise might be).

So measuring total amount of shares is very key to figuring out how many people identify with your message and trust in your brand enough to recommend it.

# II. ENGAGEMENT

As we discussed in chapter six, you need to have a way to let people know they can message you back. There needs to be a platform that they can communicate with you on. Once this is established, if you get no one messaging you, no one commenting on your platform, then you know that you're not engaging with people. If no one is responding to you, then what are the chances of them actually going and buying something that you think that they should buy?

Engagement is an indicator of trust. If you don't have engagement, then you are not developing enough trust.

## III. RESPONSE TO CALLS TO ACTION

As we've discussed, calls to action don't have to be requests to 'Buy my stuff.' They can be invitations to 'Go check out this website,' or 'Share this with a friend,' or 'Listen to the next episode,' or 'Give me a review/rating,' or 'Subscribe to my email newsletter.' You can issue multiple calls to action, ranging from very small ones to very large ones.

You need to be able to measure whether or not, and in what numbers, people are obeying these calls to action. This shows you whether or not they trust you, whether or not they believe you are asking them to do something that will be of value to them.

These are three different examples of how you can build trust metrics. You need to find a way to measure them on a regular basis and make sure that there's an upward trend. If not, then your strategy needs to change around how you go about developing trust.

## 2. RELATIONSHIP METRICS

While trust metrics are really important when you're figuring out whether your message is clear and engaging the people whom you're trying to serve, relationship metrics are really important for figuring out how well you're growing your business network.

These are the questions you need to ask yourself regularly to gather relationship metrics:

# I. HOW MANY NEW INFLUENCERS HAVE YOU MET?

Influencers are really important when it comes to business; it's all about credibility. That's why celebrities are poached to run air conditioning advertisements, even though they could be cricketers or they could be actors and they probably have nothing to do with air conditioning. It is because of the influence they have established. It enables them to lend credibility to brands that they endorse, because people care to hear from them. They care about their message.

It's no different in business. If you're in the accounting space, there will be people there who are influencers when it comes to the industry. How many of these influencers know you, or at least know who you are? If they know who you are, then chances are that their customers will know who you are as well. It's a cycle – the more influencers you know, the more you develop relationships with them, the more influence you have yourself. Developing relationships and meeting influencers is one of the most important things you should be doing as a business.

# II. HOW MANY CUSTOMERS HAVE YOU GAINED THROUGH YOUR CONTENT?

This determines the strength of the relationships that you have developed with your people. When your people aren't buying from you – and this goes back to the trust metrics I've just been through – then you're not developing enough attention, enough engagement and enough trust to bring people to buy from you. You haven't developed a relationship with them.

I mentioned the Savvy Dentist in chapter six. As I said, he told me that he can directly correlate $80,000 of business to the first twelve episodes of his podcast. He has been able to measure the value of the customers that he has converted from listeners of his content into customers. This is very powerful. It means he knows what he's doing is working. So it is important to figure out how many customers you get because of the content that you put out there.

## III. HOW MANY NEW REFERRALS HAVE YOU GOT?

Another way to measure the strength of your relationships is to consider the amount of referral business you receive from the clients you have an existing relationship with. This is where the strength of your relationships pays dividends. How many leads do you have because one of your customers has recommended your business? How many people have enquired about your product because a friend of theirs is using it?

The main thing is to keep track of your relationship metrics on a regular basis so you know exactly what you're achieving in terms of building peer and customer networks.

# 3. ANALYSIS METRICS

Analysis metrics are the ones that a lot of businesses will say you should be measuring, so these metrics are not going to come as a surprise to you as a business owner. Let's look at the ones you should be focusing on.

## I. COST OF CUSTOMER ACQUISITION

How much does it cost you to get a new client? This is the cost of acquisition, which is a really, really important metric, because if it costs you $100 to get a new client and you know that a client is going to spend $1,000 with you, then you know that you're on the right track. Your client costs are ten per cent.

## II. CUSTOMER LIFETIME VALUE

If your customer stays with you for three years and every year they spend $1,000 with you, and you spent $100 to acquire that customer, that is a great return on investment. Being able to extrapolate in order to figure this metric out will help you define your marketing efforts.

These two metrics will help you establish whether your marketing system is working for you or not. You need to know that a customer is going to do much more than merely pay off the expense of attracting them to and onboarding them with the business. If that expense is disproportionately high, then you may need a new marketing system entirely.

So these are the three types of metric that I think you should worry about as a business: trust metrics, relationship metrics and analysis metrics. I suggest that you pick a selection of metrics from each of these areas, monitor them on a dashboard, and take measurements on a weekly basis.

You will know which ones matter most to you. Look at the goals that you're trying to achieve and use them as a strategy to pick the metrics that you care about. Create a system that allows you to measure them accurately and regularly. That will make a massive difference as to what happens next. From tracking your metrics, you will see patterns and be able to monitor cause and effect when you change something.

There's a really interesting assessment by the Fournaise Marketing Group. This is a direct quote from the ROI assessment that they did: 'Nine out of ten global marketers, that's ninety per cent, are not trained to calculate return on investment and eighty per cent struggled with being able to properly demonstrate to their management the business effectiveness of their spending, campaigns and activities.'

That's a very powerful statement. That's a wake-up call telling us that we need to be paying more attention to our return on investment.

I didn't want to have a podcast for the sake of having a podcast. And I didn't want to be flying in the dark. The last thing I wanted to do was arrive six or ten months down the line and realise that all my efforts in creating a podcast were wasted, and I don't think that you want that either. There's always a strategy that can be implemented. Always a strategy that's new and novel. As a business owner, your job is to figure out what works for your business, and the best way to figure out what works for your business is by measuring the effectiveness of your strategy through a variety of different metrics.

# IMPROVING YOUR RETURN ON INVESTMENT THROUGH AUDIO

Before I end this chapter, I want to talk about a study that I found really, really interesting. It was completed by Microsoft and it used big data to measure return on investment of digital marketing, both without any traditional advertising done in conjunction, and when combined with traditional advertising. They found that digital marketing outperforms all forms of traditional advertising – television, print, radio and outdoor – while combining both methods resulted in the highest ROI. So digital marketing isn't just a strategy anymore. Businesses need to blend both traditional and digital forms of marketing, and they need to find new ways to introduce themselves on new media, because of the way that people are consuming new media. When you think about the fact that your phone is the first and last screen that you look at every single day, why wouldn't you want to have content that allows people to engage with you and your business that's available through their phone? If you think about the fact that a podcasting app cannot even be deleted off an iPhone, it tells you a lot about where they believe the medium is going.

As an added advantage, when you have an audio platform, there are further ways to leverage that in order to improve your yield. Here are a few ways you can use the fact you have a podcast to gain more return:

# 1. ADVERTISING

When you create free content, the most obvious source of revenue is to get someone to pay you money to display their message on your content, because there is going to be a bunch of people listening. Advertising has changed massively over the last decade, and the next five years are not going to be any different. The added advantage of having a podcast is that you can get a company on board that shares values with the people who are tuning in to listen to your show on a regular basis.

There are very few mediums out there that can target potential clients the way a podcast can, and it is imperative that you explain that to a potential advertiser. It isn't a billboard and it isn't a newspaper article. It is way more targeted than you can get with either one of those mediums, and, more importantly, you can get the exact numbers of how many people are listening to your show every day. There's a vast difference between telling you that my podcast Bond

Appetit is a successful show and I have a few listeners, and telling you that, as of today, 23 July 2016, Bond Appetit has 2,454,072 listeners, and those listeners exist in 133 countries around the world. Those statistics, when I say them out loud, are mind-blowing to me. When I say these numbers out loud, people understand exactly what they're getting into, as opposed to only having a vague idea. This ability to measure reach means that advertisers become very interested in what you're doing and become a source of revenue.

## 2. LISTENER CONTRIBUTIONS

When you have an audio platform, you have a bunch of listeners who are engaged with your content and care about what you're doing. So if you haven't heard about a service called Patreon, it's time that you do. Patreon is a brilliant service that allows your listeners to support your creations. As they say on their website, they give listeners the opportunity to: 'Be a Patreon of the arts. Support and engage with the creators you love.' In every episode, you can ask your listeners to support you through the smallest of contributions to help you achieve whatever goal it is that you've set out to conquer. Couple that with a crowdfunding campaign and you have a brilliant strategy to fund your next big project. This is why setting out the goals and vision for your business is important. It allows your listeners and your people to come together around this big vision that you have and participate in it.

# 3. AFFILIATE SCHEMES

When you create a podcast with a following, you know what your listeners' problems and biggest fears are. If you can see a certain product is going to make their lives easier but it's not one that you're in a position to offer yourself, then you can present them with someone else's product and pull in a referral fee. These days, it's so easy to set up the tools and put a system in place that means you have money arrive straight into your bank if someone follows a referral link to someone else's product. And when you think about it, you're really helping your people – you're solving their problems. If someone else has created a product that will allow them to solve a problem, then you don't even have to create the product. You can just approach the business that has and say, 'If my people buy the product, can I get a ten / fifteen / thirty-five / fifty per cent referral fee?' In most cases, that won't be a problem. So look at the affiliate factor when it comes to an audio platform that you create.

# 4. PROFESSIONAL SPEAKING

Having a podcast or an audio platform is a brilliant way to enter the arena of getting on stage and create a side business out of speaking. If you are a business owner looking to create waves with your personal brand, you can start hiring yourself out as a public speaker. There are so many big time public speakers who have started off with a podcast. When you're on stage presenting, you are automatically seen as an influential person within your industry. It is the ability to think on your feet and produce coherent sentences that makes you great on stage, so use a podcast to create your speaker profile and market yourself.

When you create an audio platform, these are the ways you can add return on investment to your business by taking things a step further.

So stop being naïve when it comes to where your money comes from and where it goes. Always refer back to your goals. Set up metrics and measure your yield constantly. Take advantage of the added return audio can bring you. And if you need to, adjust your strategy until you succeed.

For a worksheet to help you get a yield on your investment, go to theamplifybook.com

# WHERE TO FROM HERE

*'When I'm writing, I need to amplify my thoughts and feelings on just a conversation that I might have had with somebody - somebody close to me. It's often the case that the people closest to me are the people on my mind the most.'*

**— JAMES BAY**

**THERE ARE SEVEN** traits that businesses need to grow. If you have these seven traits, then you'll find your business growing just fine. You want your business to be:

**1. EXPRESSIBLE** – By this, I mean you are a business that knows exactly who you are, what you want, whom you're after, who your peers and potential partners are, and you are able to articulate and communicate all of these things clearly. You are able to express yourself so your business is never invisible, never overlooked.

**2. RECOGNISABLE** – You know that when someone sees your work, they say, 'Oh, this is this business. I know them. I know what they believe in. I know what they do.' You're recognisable for the nature of the work you've done because your brand shines through everything, not because your logo is slapped on an advert.

**3. SCALABLE** – You have managed to productise your ecosystem. You're able to focus on spending the right kind of energy and the right amount of time in the right places, so you can grow without having to add more people, more resources, and, therefore, encountering more costs and more issues.

**4. CONSUMABLE** – Your business has content that people come across and lap up. They don't have to make a lot of effort. They can take in your message even while they're doing other things, while they're driving their car, while they're going to the gym, while they're taking a walk, while they're mowing their lawn.

**5. MARKETABLE** – You have a message and it's loud and clear and easily spread across a variety of platforms. No one ever looks at your business, at your content, and says, 'Oh I don't understand, let me go to the next person.' They come across your authentic content on any number of different media and understand exactly what you do and they say, 'I get it and I want to check this out.'

**6. TRUSTWORTHY** – You have spent time and effort making sure that you've developed relationships with your people. They like you. They've gotten to know you. There are enough ways for people to come into contact with and connect with your brand that they can see you mean what you say and keep your promises.

**7. MEASURABLE** – Your business understands exactly where you're putting your efforts so you are able to measure success using reliable metrics, meaning you're able to manage the results and improve on them.

These are the seven traits a business needs in order to grow. I've just taken you through the AMPLIFY framework which instills these traits in your business and makes growth both possible and sustainable. We've talked about the importance of analysing your audience, moulding your brand, productising your ecosystem, launching audio, intensifying your message, fostering engagement and yielding return on all that investment. Put together, you've learned how to gain fifteen times the impact with one tenth the effort.

So now what?

Wherever your business goes from here, keep amplifying it. Get more out of your people. Get more out of your peers. Get more out of yourself.

Following are some final pieces of advice to help you amplify your business.

# AMPLIFY YOUR AUDIENCE

I believe that there is one major way to amplify your audience, and that's to tell stories.

We love real stories. We love authenticity. Let's talk about Humans of New York – there's Humans of Everything these days. The idea has been amplified because of the success of Humans of New York. Brandon Stanton is the photographer and creator who has documented life on the streets of New York for six years now. What he does is photograph people every day and tell their stories. These stories range from inspiring to heartbreaking, and people love to follow them. The impact of Humans of New York has been so massive that he has been able to raise money for a variety of different causes, including Brooklyn school children. This all came from a photograph that he took of a young boy who said that his school principal was the most influential person in his life. He went to talk to the principal of the school in Brownsville, Brooklyn, which has the city's highest crime rate, and found that it had a tough neighbourhood with a whole bunch of issues. So he decided to raise money and take it to a new level, which was possible because of the reach that he has with Humans of New York. The reason he has this reach is that he has over a million followers looking to find out what the next story is. The stories are brilliant.

So to amplify your own audience, find some stories to share with them that they'll want to share themselves. Serial the podcast got so much fame because it's a real story told in a real, authentic way.

People are captivated by the story. That's why television series work. That's why movies work. Stories are imperative for creating shareable content.

# AMPLIFY YOUR PARTNERSHIPS

In chapter one, when we spoke about audience analysis, we went into detail about how important our peers are. But how do you create more peers? How do you create more partnerships? You've got to look at the people who share the audience that you're after. Always be looking to see what your people do on either side of engaging with your business. That's when you can find out which people you should create partnerships with. And keep up to date with the changes in your industry – there will always be new players entering your space. Chances are, if you can create partnerships with them, and there's no competitive overlap, they won't have an issue advertising you and your services to their people.

Are you getting your partners to introduce you to other potential partners? If you are interviewing people on your audio platform, are you asking them, at the end of the recording, whether there are other people they think you should interview? Or other people they think could contribute to your particular industry? Amplifying your partnerships is one of the easiest ways to amplify your business.

# AMPLIFY YOUR SUCCESS

Having a process is the key to getting things done right. Let me give you the example of a cup of tea. I have a certain tea that I like and I like it made in a certain way – it's green tea with lime. I know that when I make my cup of tea, I like the green tea to be steeped in boiling water for ten minutes, with one whole lime squeezed into the brew. That's what I consider my perfect cup of green tea. Now, if I didn't tell you that and I just said, 'Could you make me a cup of green tea with lime?' then you wouldn't know exactly what it is that I want. However, if I gave you a set of steps and defined the process of making me that cup of tea, I would get close to or even exactly the same cup of tea that I like to enjoy.

It takes a quality process to get a quality product – this is an idea I've written a thesis on. So I think to amplify your success, you need to create a quality process. Once you're achieving results, think about how you can document your processes in such a way as to make it possible to give them to someone else to replicate. The more processes you're able to get off your plate, the more you can focus on higher tasks that will take you even further, towards even bigger goals.

So once you have the framework working for you, focus on amplifying your audience, your partnerships and your success – you'll take your business to a whole other level.

You will find a whole bunch of worksheets and additional material if you go to theamplifybook.com. But if you have just finished this book thinking, 'Maybe I should start a podcast,' then you need to go to ShouldIStartAPodcast.com and pick some episodes that you find interesting. I interview podcasters who have been around the block and the show will give you enough of an insight into the wide world of podcasting for you to make an informed decision.

# ABOUT RONSLEY

*Written by Andrew Griffiths, Australia's #1 Small Business and Entrepreneurial Author – with 12 books sold in over 60 countries.*

Ronsley is certainly one of a kind. Over the last few years I've thoroughly enjoyed getting to know him, appreciate the way his mind works and the way he looks at the world. Being a modest kind of fella, he asked me to write the 'About Ronsley' section of his book, which I'm pretty darn happy to do.

The place to start is to acknowledge Ronsley's brain – it's big. He's got an MBA in Psychology and Leadership, a Master's in Software Engineering and a Diploma in Financial Services. In amongst this he's collected a variety of designations, which include software engineer, software quality manager, tutor and financial advisor. This background is reflected in the way Ronsley works – he is methodical, a very deep thinker, clearly strategic in all he does and very logical (he's kinda like an Indian Spock).

His other side is a restaurateur, chef, entrepreneur, bartender, podcaster, speaker and, now, author.

I see Ronsley as the perfect storm of technical intelligence, passionate thinking, new world communication and extraordinary podcasting. The one thing that impresses me the most is the way he challenges the status quo in all he does. Ronsley is always the one in the room who makes a suggestion out of the blue that stops the conversation and gives everyone something 'big' to ponder. Every meeting, brainstorming, strategy and planning session needs a Ronsley.

Today, his podcast Bond Appetit is huge. With close to three million listeners in over 130 countries, Ronsley has dived in to the world of audio to reach audiences. Of course starting a podcast wasn't enough. He also founded the largest annual podcast conference in the southern hemisphere, 'We are Podcast', which attracts people from around the world to learn more about this phenomenal medium.

To top this, Ronsley has recently launched Australia's first audio marketing agency – AMPLIFY. His totally unique range of services are all designed to help businesses, large and small, to harness the power of conversation to market themselves more effectively across a range of mediums. I use his services and they are, as expected, awesome.

So that is Ronsley. But to be honest, that's just a little bit of him. The man I have grown to know and love has an enormous heart that he shares with those around him. He's a compassionate human being with a huge desire to make the world a better place and he is always quick to laugh in one second and then ask the really hard questions the next.

My prediction is that you, like me, will be reading (and listening to) a lot more about Ronsley Seriojo Vaz in the coming years.

Connect with Ronsley on these channels:

- Connect with Ronsley on Facebook: facebook.com/ronsley

- Connect with Ronsley on Twitter: twitter.com/ronsley

- Connect with We Are Podcast on Instagram: instagram.com/wearepodcast

- Go to the We Are Podcast website: wearepodcast.com

- Go to the Amplify website: mustamplify.com

- Listen to 'Should I Start a Podcast?': ShouldIStartaPodcast.com

- Listen to the 'Bond Appetit' podcast: bond-appetit.com

www.ingramcontent.com/pod-product-compliance
Lightning Source LLC
Chambersburg PA
CBHW042313210326
41598CB00042B/7373